THE PATH OF LIFE

THE PATH OF LIFE

KEN STALLARD

Matador
Unit E2 Airfield Business Park,
Harrison Road, Market Harborough,
Leicestershire. LE16 7UL
Tel: 0116 279 2299
Email: books@troubador.co.uk
Web: www.troubador.co.uk/matador
Twitter: @matadorbooks

ISBN 978 1803136 110

British Library Cataloguing in Publication Data.
A catalogue record for this book is available from the British Library.

Printed and bound in Great Britain by 4edge Limited
Typeset in 11pt Minion by Troubador Publishing Ltd, Leicester, UK

Matador is an imprint of Troubador Publishing Ltd

*Dedicated to the glory of God
and to all travellers with me on the path of life.*

Thou wilt show me THE PATH OF LIFE: in Thy Presence is fullness of joy, at Thy right hand there are pleasures for ever more.

Psalm 16 verse 11

ONE

I find it very hard to acknowledge that I have been an evangelist in a Christian ministry for sixty years. Six decades of learning and still constantly gaining new skills in the ministry.

One thing that is constant and never changes is that God in Jesus Christ is forever the same. Although folk seem to be forever trying to modernise God, it will never happen.

When God said, "For I am the Lord, I change not," in Malachi 3 verse 6 He meant it. Even the writer to Hebrews Chapter 13 verse 8 declares, "Jesus Christ the same yesterday, and today and forever."

Hardly a month goes by without someone saying, "You *are* old fashioned," or, "Ken, when are you going to get modern and catch up with the twenty-first century?" My answer is always the same: "I serve an old-fashioned God. I have an old-fashioned gospel with an old-fashioned faith!" God never changes and I do not intend to.

The Bible, which I believe is God's infallible Word, is not for changing either. Generations have attempted to change the Bible. Many have tried to update the meaning or explain away the very fundamentals of the sacred text. Clearly these folk fail to understand what God means when He says, "If any man shall take away from the words of the book of this prophecy, God shall take away his part out of the book of life, and out of the holy city, and from the things which are written in this book." At the very end of the Bible we have that warning in the last but three verses. It is just as though He is saying, "That is my final word on the matter."

I never cease to be amazed how modern folk complain that the Bible is too hard to understand. This doesn't say very much for this modern age of technology and added years of education and wisdom. When we think how folk were converted and became God-fearing from back in the seventeenth century. Some knew far more then with little or no schooling. Many could not read or write. Such people were blessed with good ears for listening and a willingness to learn.

The problem why so many people find the Bible is too difficult to understand is because of their approach to it. If we start reading it as a normal book we shall not understand it because it is supernatural.

The Bible gives us its own explanation in 1 Corinthians Chapter 2 verse 14: "But the natural man receiveth not the things of the Spirit of God: for they are foolishness unto him: neither can he know them, because they are spiritually discerned."

When we approach the Bible we need to be spiritually aware so that God can speak to us through what we read. It is advisable, therefore, to pray that God will reveal what He wants us to know and experience. "That the God of our Lord Jesus Christ, the Father of glory, may give unto you the spirit of wisdom and revelation in the knowledge of Him." Ephesians Chapter 1 verse 17.

2

There have never been so many "versions" of the Bible as in the past fifty years. Clearly some of them are blatant "perversions" that contradict and confuse the reader.

Although I often compare newer versions for a broader view of scriptural context, I never depart from the King James Version for preaching and for use in the pulpit. In my opinion the beautiful English form of language is much easier to memorise texts than trying to remember modern sentences. With sixty years of experience I have found the KJV to be reliable and tried and tested. Our predecessors were converted by what they heard from it. They understood the contents of Romans Chapter 10 verse 17: "So then faith cometh by hearing, and hearing by the word of God."

So, starting out on this Christian path of life I set out on my journey with the very basis of three essential requirements. First, belief in the Persons of God, Jesus Christ His Son and the Holy Spirit. Second, to have unshakeable faith that these Three Persons will never leave or forsake me for time and eternity. Thirdly, there are miracles and amazing experiences all along the way.

I could never have visualised the promise of God's Word penned by the writer of Hebrews Chapter 11 verse 6: "But without faith it is impossible to please Him: for He that cometh to God must believe that He is, and that He is a rewarder of them that diligently seek Him." I discover that every single day of my life.

Two

My very earliest memories are going with my mum and little baby sister to see Granny at Uffington. This was a delightful village nestling in the valley of the famous White Horse Hill in very rural Berkshire. Uffington was midway between the small market towns of Wantage, also famous for being the birthplace of King Alfred the Great, and Faringdon.

It was at least two miles from where we were living at a little hamlet called Baulking Grange. The hamlet consisted of half a dozen farm cottages which were owned by a farmer whose farm was situated on the other side of the road. Dad was a farm labourer at the farm. The main Great Western Railway ran from Didcot to Swindon through the meandering meadows beside the farm.

The highlights of my life involved visits to Granny, which took place most afternoons. Seven days a week Dad would go after lunch time to get in a large herd of cows for milking. This gave Mum the opportunity to bring out the old pram and wrap up baby sister Peggy for conveying her and myself to Uffington. I used to run beside the pram some of the way, but when I got weary, Mum would stick me in beside Peggy in the pram. That couple of miles each way were challenging when it poured with rain.

Perhaps the very first memory I have concerns returning home to Baulking Grange after the customary visit to see Granny. I was aware that something strange was happening to us that day.

As Peggy snuggled up in the pram and I was walking alongside we passed Baulking Vicarage. The vicar's wife came out and seemed very agitated as she called to my mother.

"Oh dear! Lily," she said. "Get those children home and indoors as soon as you can. The air-raid siren is on and there are a couple of German aircraft coming."

Mum scooped me up and planked me beside my sister in the pram. She started running, gasping, and muttering, "Oh no," as she ran as fast as she could. The pram rocked from side to side and I liked it. Years later, whenever Mum recalled that afternoon, she said I was laughing hysterically and kept saying, "Run some more, Mum, run some more," whenever she slowed down to get her breath back.

A world war meant nothing to such a small child, but within a few months later I became very aware that something was very wrong and things were different at home.

It was Christmas Day and I was looking forward to a visit from Father Christmas and hopefully a gift of a magic colouring book. I loved to pop my brush into a jam jar full of clear water, and when you transferred the brush to the paper, the coloured pictures appeared on the pages.

This Christmas Day didn't seem right and I could not understand why Mum kept weeping and Dad kept whispering. Some relatives came in to see us and they seemed to be giving me more attention than usual. The thing I could not understand was, where was my sister?

Dad eventually sat me down and explained that we would not be seeing my sister anymore because it was Christmas Day and Peggy had gone to Heaven.

Although I could not understand why it was necessary for Peggy to go and be with the angels on such a special day, I accepted what Dad said and just hoped that he and Mum would not be upset for too long.

Not many weeks later Dad decided to quit the job and sought another farm-labouring job at another hamlet which only housed a farmhouse and three farm cottages. This time it was called Moor Mill but still only a couple of miles from Uffington but in the opposite direction.

There was no electricity in the cottages or indoor water supply. We had no luxury of a bathroom and very little farm wage to live on. Our lighting existed of old oil lamps with tall thin glass coverings which often cracked or broke when cold draughts blew onto the heated glass. Mum cooked on a twin paraffin cooker where one small oven perched on top of one of the flames. The small kitchen always wafted of cooking and paraffin fumes.

In winter months, especially during frosts and snow, my dad would put a bale of straw around the outdoor frozen tap and set fire to it so that it could thaw out. We carried buckets of water indoors to fill a big tin bath every Sunday for the one bath a week. We all used the same water.

Moor Mill was extremely quiet with only elderly neighbours in the two other cottages apart from our own. There were no other children for me to play with. The only bright side was that Mum continued to take me to see Granny most days. The pram had long fallen to pieces and so Mum strapped me on the back of an ancient bicycle and pedalled me to and fro Uffington.

The following year three big events happened at Moor Mill. A German aircraft attempted to bomb a train and Dad took us to see a massive crater in one of the adjacent fields. Later on my dad was the first on the scene when another German aeroplane crashed in another of the fields and an ambulance took the dead pilot away. I remember Mum taking me to see bunches of flowers which local folk had placed near the wreck of the aircraft.

The third big event was the best of all. I was brought downstairs in my pyjamas and propped up in a load of pillows in a very large winged chair in our kitchen. Dad took the nurse upstairs and then informed me that I was going to have another little new sister. I saw the nurse coming in and she spoke to me as she carried a very large bag and I presumed the baby was inside. Sister Audrey had arrived!

I suppose on reflection there was nothing very special or significant about Moor Mill. That little tiny corner in Berkshire. It was not even considered for promotion when the area slipped into a new boundary and became Oxfordshire. It was really no more than a change of status and nothing different had changed. However, within months it had become to me the greatest place in the whole wide world.

Having travelled twice around the globe and visited and ministered in three dozen countries ever since, it was, and still is, my favourite place in the whole wide world outside of Heaven.

Three

When the war ended Dad seemed to be more busy than ever. He was always busy around the farm, and when that was not occupying his time, he was industrious in numerous hobbies and pastimes.

Some evenings he was out with other young men serving in the Home Guard. Guarding and keeping us safe at little Moor Mill was hardly a national priority in his view. There were many other things to attend to.

Indoors our only luxury, apart from the wide open-fireplace full of massive logs burning and crackling on cold dark evenings, was our old wireless set. The wooden box affair was rigged up to a large high-tension battery attached to a heavy accumulator full of acid. To preserve the short accumulator and battery life the wireless was only used when some special programme was being aired. It was usually the national news, comedy shows and especially every Saturday night's play.

I learnt at a very young age to be an avid listener because there was very little else to do.

Dad was engaged in many pursuits, usually because he took advantage of what the war afforded. I would snuggle up into the old wing chair and listen to what my parents were discussing. Most of it, I now admit, was not really a good influence on a child of about seven years of age.

I enjoyed the chats. It was fascinating to hear how Dad had found an abandoned parachute in some trees at the back of our houses. That had been bundled off to the public house near the railway station. The Junction pub was a popular venue to offload anything in exchange for a bit of much-needed cash.

The parachute was bought by a couple who wanted the silk so that the daughter could get a wedding dress made with it when clothing coupons were in short supply. Every time Dad went to the Junction or the White Horse at Uffington he had something to sell. He would take no end of vegetables from the garden that he worked on, and never-ending potatoes, lettuces and plums or apples from trees at the bottom of the garden.

When produce and vegetables got short of supply Dad went off rabbiting. This was his very popular pastime and involved taking one of his pet ferrets, which he released into rabbit holes in the fields. He must have been good at what he was doing because he always had some rabbits he caught to sell at the pub and to the locals.

Back at home we kept chickens and I loved to go around the nests to collect eggs.

Mum kept us going with baked rabbit pie, stewed rabbit, rabbit soup, endless apple pies and blackberry jam in season from the berries from the hedgerows around the farm. She also kept nagging at Dad to get another pram because now she had Audrey and myself to take on the excursions to Granny. She could no longer carry two children on one bicycle. We were eventually rewarded with a pram that Dad put together from odd parts.

In retrospect I realise that although my father was very hard-working and devoted to the family, he was not very patient and would often fly into a rage if something wasn't to his liking. I saw some fights he would have with Mum and bad arguments that they had together.

Sometimes I would lay in bed and hear Mum and Dad shouting and quarrelling downstairs. I was terrified and pulled the blankets over my head to shut out the sound. When there was a lull in the arguing, or when it went quiet, I was fearful that one had killed the other.

I recall this as a very difficult time for me as I was growing older. I began to be fearful about Dad and his temper. My grandad died a short time after Audrey was born, but she was far too young even to remember him. Granny, therefore, loved to have any, and quite often, opportunities for me to stay with her for a few days at a time, because without Grandpa she was very lonely. I adored staying with her.

During the next year Dad changed his job three times. We moved once after being in one cottage for only a month. It was always to different agricultural homes and farms near to where Granny lived.

It was during one of my stints of living with Gran that I was introduced to a neighbour's son who was exactly one year younger than me. He was also called Ken. We became very good friends and we were constantly at each other's homes. During one of his visits Ken invited me to go to a Sunday school at a congregational non-conformist evangelical chapel in Granny's village.

The prospect filled me with eager anticipation because normal schooling was rather foreign to me. Schools were at least a couple of walking miles each way from home. Dad seemed to be constantly working at different farms in isolated places far from school. The constant upheaval was very unsettling. No sooner were arrangements made for my school attendance than the policy was changed. It would be a different school, or a different job, or yet another home. It became more non-attendance than an option for my education.

Yes, I looked forward to going to the chapel Sunday school. I thought it would be good to learn to read and write there, and I wondered about play times?

I was very overwhelmed with my first visit, even though I was very warmly welcomed by two middle-aged sisters whom I shall call Nancy and Elsie.

There was no playground, although there must have been at least thirty pupils in the Sunday school.

Elsie played the organ and Nancy led us in singing, but I did not know the song and I could not read the words. I just hummed along the best as I could.

I was completely baffled when we all sat down and we were told to put our hands together and look up at the ceiling with our eyes closed. I could not understand why "Auntie" spoke to the ceiling, or why we had to call Nancy "Auntie" because she really wasn't our auntie, and we didn't have any writing or sums. I understood a little better when that faithful servant explained that they were not speaking to the ceiling, but they were "praying", whatever that meant.

Before Elsie played the organ again Auntie Nancy told us a lovely tale about Jesus. She was very gifted at storytelling and told us that Jesus is really alive. I learnt that day that He had done many wonderful things; indeed, He had performed many miracles, but now He was up in Heaven with His Father, God!

Auntie Nancy was so convincing about Jesus and how much we need to know Him. Although we cannot see Jesus face to face, Auntie explained, we can know He is there and when she was praying she was actually speaking to Jesus. That is why they were looking up. Not speaking to the ceiling, as I thought, but praying to Jesus, who is far up higher than the rafters. Living up there in Heaven with God, His Heavenly Father.

"Remember, children," Aunt Elsie enthused. "Remember, children, God always answers every prayer!" I was greatly impressed. Not more so than that very afternoon when I had walked all the way back home to Moor Mill.

As was usual, Dad was sleeping in his chair beside the hearth. It was a ritual to him. The pattern was the same every Sunday afternoon. First lunch, sleep by the fireside, then getting up to go off to herd up the cows for milking before teatime. I never ventured to go in and disturb Dad when he was sleeping, which would be very much to my cost. Instead, I wandered aimlessly around the farm and came across a very interesting sight.

Two large, panelled gates with a cross bar kept from view whatever was behind. Curiosity got the better of me and I decided to investigate further and eased out the cross bar and opened the gates. Inside there was a herd of cows.

No sooner had I opened the gates than the cows began running towards me and I was terrified. I ran off, and to my horror the cows kept on running behind me until the leaders saw a gap in the hedge and ran through it. I immediately saw that they were trampling down high ripened corn in the field. I was terrified. I knew that as soon as my dad had found out what I had done, he would be so cross and I would be severely punished.

At that precise moment Auntie Elsie's words came to mind: "Remember, children, God always answers every prayer!" Never did I ever feel so much the need of a prayer to be answered as at that precise moment. I wonder why so many people only ever pray when they are afraid or facing a crisis?

I knew there was nothing whatsoever I could do with the problem of the escaped cows but to pray. I went into the far side of a very large field and beside a brook I knelt down under an enormous pear tray and stammered out my prayer.

"Please, God, I believe in You. Please do me a favour and get the cows out of the field and I will not get into trouble." It was a short but a very direct prayer, watered by my tears. At that moment I expected God to do something.

He did!

As I stood to my feet I saw an amazing sight. I watched in awe as about twenty cows started ambling towards the wide gap in the hedge and came through it and into the road. Instinctively they wandered towards the open gate to the yard and every one went back inside from whence they had left.

I was full of different emotions, but the most dramatic was seeing how the cows moved. The whole episode was so orderly, but what amazed me most of all was the fact that I could not see where any corn had been trampled down.

I knew I had had an experience with God and I had seen with my own eyes a miracle.

No-one knew what I had done. No-one else had seen the miracle. Not a living soul had ever witnessed what I had just seen. To me that was a divine appointment with God. It was our secret.

God must be so Mighty and Wonderful and obviously not too busy to hear the cry of a small boy in such an isolated place.

Looking back on that first miracle nowadays it helps me to understand what the Bible says when I read in Hebrews Chapter 11 and verse 6: "But without faith it is impossible to please Him: for he that cometh to God must believe that He is, and that He is a rewarder of them that diligently seek Him."

Four

My secret with God was phenomenal. It had such a profound effect upon me. For days following the encounter with the cows in the corn, I kept going back to see the place where the miracle had taken place. There was nothing special to see and everything looked just the same.

I decided I would not tell anyone what I had experienced. It was too wonderful for me. I decided that God might not want me to tell what He did in secret, and if I did He might be angry with me and not do any more miracles for me.

At the front of our cottage was a very old upended grass roller with shafts and a cross bar of wood. There was so little to do at Moor Mill, but every day I would make my way to that roller. I would stand on the roller and run my fingers over the wooden cross bar. I saw the bar as my organ and I pretended to play it every day. It was my way of being still in contact with God and I wanted to stay close in case I needed Him again.

At the back of the three row of cottages was the cow yard and beyond that a couple of very large barns. There were roofs and side boards to the barns but no windows or doors. The fronts were large open spaces.

There were also at least a couple of wagons or trailers in these barns. They were very simple wooden affairs with rubber tyres, usually used for carrying corn or grass and hay and quite often for manure.

Almost on a daily basis I would go out to the fields and pick bunches of buttercups and cow parsley. I would gather an armful to decorate the front two corners of one of the trailers. Then, when decoration was complete, I would stand in the front of the mounted trailer and preach to the chickens scratching in the straw nearby.

Most Sunday mornings my mother's sister, Innie, would come to us at Moor Mill on an old bicycle to see how we were. She was called "Innie", a nickname that she had been left with from her baby days. Her name was Winifred or Winnie, but because she could not pronounce her "W"s she was stuck with "Innie" for the rest of her life.

Living in Oxford during the week Innie came to spend time with Granny most weekends.

Innie was very impressed when she cycled to Moor Mill to give me the weekly three penny bit pocket money and found me in my trailer come pulpit.

When she went indoors she joked with my mum. "I reckon he will be a preacher one day," she prophesied.

I continued to go to the Congregational Chapel at Uffington most Sunday afternoons even when Ken, who had taken me there in the first place, stopped attending.

I had grown very fond of Aunty Nancy and Elsie, who were not only extremely kind but also very encouraging. They taught me a lot of stories from the Bible and I tried to learn as much as I could about Jesus. After all, I mused, I had had a real experience of knowing Him. Only once in all the years did I ever see Aunty Nancy and Elsie being very cross with me on a single occasion.

Often the very large chapel black-leaded Tortoise stove used for heating would play up. Newspaper and kindling wood were based at the bottom of the stove and then when the paper was lit with a match and it began to burn, some coal was added and then this was topped up with coke. It was not unusual that the fire would go out sometimes before the wood caught and the chapel would be filled with smoke. I could see how frustrated the aunties would get most weeks and so one Sunday I decided to help out.

When Auntie wasn't looking I popped in a camp coffee bottle of paraffin into the top of the stove. We had a lot of it at home because Mum used it for cooking and lighting. I knew she would not miss a bottle-full. The result was terrifying. There was a loud explosion; the crash of breaking glass and massive flames shot out of both the top and flue apertures of the stove. The children laughed and thought it was great fun, but our teachers were not impressed. It was the only time I had seen them annoyed and I was severely reprimanded.

Almost needless to say Dad got bored with working on the Moor Mill farm. He gave notice of leaving when the farmer had asked him to do some job on the farm which he refused to do. Consequently he got another farm-labouring job on another farm, but there was no tied cottage which went with the job. We went to live with Granny at her house, but I knew it would only be temporary because Dad would be looking for work elsewhere and he did. We moved on several times and back and forwards to live with Granny as the need arose. I guess we would have continued that way of life until a farmer came to seek out my father to work for him. Although Dad had a reputation that he would not stay in a job for long, he also had great recommendation of being a very hard and industrious worker. It worked and for the first time ever we moved into a council house eight miles away in a charming little village called West Hanney. This was far superior than farm cottages with the added joy of having indoor water and electricity.

My dear long-suffering mum could not conceal her joy. She knew now that however many times Dad decided to leave his farm jobs, we would no longer be forced out of tied farm cottages that went with the job. We had a permanent home.

Surprisingly too Dad decided to give up farm work to become a builder's labourer on building sites because he said the wages were better. He continued to do this until the day he died.

Now I was living at West Hanney it had come very well to the time for me to start going out to work myself. With so little education, and because of the frequent moving from one area to another and changes of schools, I had no qualifications for anything. Writing was a problem and when I wanted to write the number of our house I was unable to write the figure 3. When I tried my mum said, "You are cack-handed and you are doing it upside down." I didn't know then what cack-handed meant but I learnt since that it means clumsy or awkward. My attempt of writing a 3 just came out looking like an "m". Mum said it looked like a bird in flight. When I arrived at the secondary school at Wantage I certainly wasn't very bright, but I knew my remaining weeks there would soon pass by.

My fifteenth birthday fell during the school Easter holiday. Mum saw that the International Stores, a country-wide country grocery shop, was advertising for staff, and I presented myself before the manager. I was duly accepted as an "all-rounder" which later my dad called a "dogsbody" which seemed to be a colloquial expression for being a jack of all trades but master of none. I was quite proud of the fact that I had got myself a job, but it seemed ironic that I never did have an official day for leaving school or saying farewell. I had a very bad bout of mumps which delayed my start at the shop by a fortnight.

God, as from the beginning, was already working His purposes out in my life even though by that time I had stopped thinking of, or serving, Him. Living at West Hanney had stopped my regular visits to the chapel and liaison with the aunties at Uffington. I had stopped praying to God and I had vacated my trailer pulpit at Moor Mill because we had left the hamlet. In my mind I was simply a teenager and I had naturally moved on to other things.

It was necessary to bike the four miles to Wantage from the day I started working at the International Stores and I thought fate had drifted my way. On the very first morning as I was cycling past a house in the neighbouring village of East Hanney a young lady came from her house on a bicycle and started cycling beside me. I discovered that she worked at a chemist in the town and we could be company for each other as we cycled to and fro work. Her named was Sue. Sue was quick to tell me that she was a Christian and that she attended the local village evangelical chapel every Sunday, to which I would be very warmly invited.

Every Sunday I promised Sue I would see her at the chapel but told her lies and made excuses every Monday morning as to why I had not turned up as promised. The real reason was because I loved the cinema and Sunday-night visits to the Regent Cinema every Sunday evening was far more exciting.

God is a patient God and amazingly Sue never gave up with the chapel invitations. Patience was finally rewarded. I had no money on a particular evening and, rather than stay at home because I didn't have money for the cinema, I decided to turn up at the chapel. Sue was delighted.

I was very impressed by all the folk in the small congregation. It was very similar to what I had been used to when I had met aunties at their very similar chapel. The difference was that this chapel had a full-time minister whom most people called affectionately "Uncle George". Who eventually turned out to be the most wonderful friend I could ever have known.

I began to enjoy the company of the Christian folk at every Sunday service. Uncle George was a great preacher and seemed to make the Bible come alive to me. It was the love of the chapel folk that meant so very much to me. I was taught the meaning of Jesus's words St. John Chapter 13 verse 35: "By this shall all men know that you are my disciples, if you have love one to another." The experience was far more interesting and exciting than anything I had ever encountered at the cinema. My friends at the chapel suddenly got very excited when they heard that the American evangelist Dr. Billy Graham was coming to England to conduct a Christian Crusade and Missions in major cities. My friend Sue and the chapel folk invited them on a coach trip to Wembley Stadium and I was very much looking forward to the event. Unbeknown to me, all the congregation were earnestly praying that I would go and that I would be responsive to God's love and His challenging Word through Dr. Graham's preaching.

It was a most wonderful meeting and I was deeply moved through the entire service. When Billy Graham gave the appeal to come and receive Jesus I just longed to respond, but I did not.

I saw many people walking down the aisles, including several airmen in uniform, to be met by counsellors who prayed with folk who had gone forward. I longed to be among them. My feet were itching to go down to the turf at Wembley Stadium and receive Jesus as my Saviour, but I was too afraid.

I looked at all the thousands of people who were sat in stands and the Wembley turf seemed so long away. Although I was so much wanting to go forward, so many nagging doubts came into my mind. I thought that I would get separated by the rest of the coach party. I was fearful of being lost and unable to find the coach in so vast a crowd. I felt innerly disappointed, but I was afraid of being separated from the best of the party. I decided it would be safer to stay with my friends.

Needless to say I realise now how much the enemy, the devil, did not want me to go and seek God's forgiveness, I knew I needed to repent of the sins in my life. I desperately want to go and receive Jesus as my Saviour, but I was overtaken by my fear and insecurity. The Bible Proverbs Chapter 29 verse 25 clearly points out, "The fear of man bringeth a snare: but whoso putteth his trust in the Lord shall be safe."

It took ages for us all as a group to find the coach for coming home. The folk seemed quiet and nowhere near as excited as they were when we went to Wembley. It took just over a week for me to find out the reason why.

They had all been praying so much that my visit to the Billy Graham Crusade would prove to be my "day of salvation", but they were disappointed that it was not so.

It is amazing that so often we try to plan God's timetable. We take on ourselves the work of the Holy Spirit. On this occasion God spoke to us through Isaiah Chapter 55 verses 8 and 9: "For my thoughts are not your thoughts, neither are your ways my ways, saith the Lord. For as the heavens are higher than the earth, so are my ways higher than your ways, and my thoughts than your thoughts."

I recall Auntie's words to us all that very first day I attend the Sunday school. They were very specific. "Remember, children, God always answers every prayer." The emphasis is on the word always.

I am still amazed that so many Christian friends share with me matters that they are praying about. Even more amazed that they say, "God has not answered our prayers." This is totally untrue and dishonouring to the Almighty. We say God has not answered our prayers when we have not received what we have asked for. We totally overlook that He answered with, "No," because His way for us is best. Possibly He has said, "Wait," because the present time is not right or He has something better in store for us than we realise. Of course, there are so many times that He says, "Yes," and grants our heart's desire. Our Lord Jesus Who is always on hand to be with the widow, the orphan and a friend Who sticketh closer than a brother, will never leave or forsake us. We can never slow the Lord down or rush Him along.

He is Perfect and His timing is always perfect too.

The very Sunday following our coach trip to the Billy Graham Crusade at Wembley was my spiritual birthday. It was the day I was "born again" into God's family, the day of my salvation. The greatest day of my entire life.

Five

Uncle George preached from St. John Chapter 3 outling the story of Nicodemus, a ruler of the Jews, who came to Jesus with searching questions about being saved. From the first day that I joined the chapel, I was taught the absolute necessity of needing salvation. I understood this to mean being delivered from sin and its consequences to be brought about with faith in Jesus.

When he got to verse 16, Uncle George read, "For God so loved the world that He gave His only begotten Son, that whosoever believeth in Him should not perish, but have everlasting life."

At this point Uncle George described about Jesus hanging on the Cross being crucified for our sins. I closed my eyes tightly as I listened to the description.

Jesus was forced to bear a crown of thorns on His brow. Compelled to be nailed through His hands and feet to that cruel Cross. Then, as though that was not enough suffering, one of the soldiers with a spear pierced His side, and forthwith there came out Blood and water.

Then I had the vision.

In my mind, even with my eyes tightly closed, I could see so plainly Jesus suffering on that Cross. It was so unlike any pictures in Bibles or illustrations I had ever seen in Scripture books. The sight still remains so vivid to this day.

Jesus's head was bowed and I saw Blood across His forehead. Blood dripped from His hands and feet, but it was His face that touched my heart.

With His head bowed there looked what I can only describe as a large bruise below His right eye. His face looked dirty. I could see so clearly two white lines in the dirt or dust where I saw the tears running down His face. I saw at once so much suffering. So much love. I knew instantly that Jesus loved me and that He was suffering for my sins and for my salvation.

As my own tears began to flow as I beheld the vision, Jesus lifted up His head and whispered one word, "Ken," and the vision immediately disappeared. Jesus had called me by name. I was prostrate and my heart felt ready to jump out of my body. Uncle George invited me into the very small vestry at the side of the chapel and said, "I believe God has spoken to you tonight." I confirmed that was so, and there and then I prayed for forgiveness for my sin. I repented because I believe without repentance there cannot be salvation. That night I accepted Jesus as my personal Saviour.

It was such a wonderful experience and two wonderful truths were presented to me instantly. First from Uncle George.

"Remember you are now born again," he said. "Born by adoption into God's family. He is a King so as a member of His Royal Family you are a Prince of His Blood Royal. Never forget who you are and Whom you serve." Then at that instant dear Brother George seemed much nearer to me than the customary "Uncle George", because he was now my brother in Christ. He then read to me from St. John Chapter 5 verse 24: "Truly, truly, I say unto you. He that heareth my Word, and believeth on Him that sent me, hath everlasting life, and shall not come into condemnation; but is passed from death unto life." My salvation is so dependent upon Jesus. Because of Him I have passed from spiritual death to life, and the penalty of sin to the glories which shall be revealed another day in Heaven.

The second encouragement was given to me by a young man who pressed a Bible into my hand. "Here is God's guarantee," he said as he opened the Bible. "Remember what God says in it and He will do it. It is necessary to read and believe and trust what He says to you through it."

I had to admit that reading the Bible would be difficult because it was outside of my capability. With my lack of education and struggling to write a figure 3 so that it didn't look like a letter "m", I wondered how I could cope with reading the Bible.

As in answer to my thoughts the young man continued. "Pray," he emphasised. "Think of what Jesus says here in St. Matthew Chapter 7 verse 7." And he quoted, "Ask, and it shall be given you; seek, and you shall find; knock, and it shall be opened unto you." I scurried off home to put this into practice immediately.

That night I read through all twenty-four chapters of St. Luke. Just as Jesus turned ordinary water into refreshing wine by His first recorded miracle, so He laid the reading of His Word upon my heart. The more I read the easier I knew what the Scripture was saying. I was reluctant to lay myself down to read in case when I woke up it was unreal and it would only be a dream. Joyfully that was not the case.

The experience of the Lord opening up the Scripture in St. Luke came dramatically when I read Chapter 5 verse 4: "Now when Jesus had left speaking, He said unto Simon, launch out into the deep, and let down your nets for a draught."

I saw the truth of the verse as though it had leapt at me from the page. I realised that the Lord was teaching me to go fishing for souls. He was urging me to launch out into the deep parts of the sea where the fish are. Too many folk seek to paddle at the water's edge with one foot on the beach and the other only ankle deep in the sea. For this reason Jesus in St. Luke Chapter 16 verse 13 said, "No servant can serve two masters; for either he will hate the one, and love the other; or else he will hold to the one, and despise the other. You cannot serve God and mammon." Here mammon speaks of wealth regarded as an evil influence of or false object of worship.

That single verse of Scripture, St. Luke Chapter 5 verse 4, concerning fishing also prompts us to let down nets plural rather just a single net. Suggesting that a draught or a number of fish can be caught. To achieve this we need to prepare and toil sometimes all night if necessary.

In the following verse 5, Simon, the fisherman, said to Jesus, "Master, we have toiled all the night, and have taken nothing: nevertheless at your word I will let down the net." We learn two very important lessons here. First not to give up too easily but be obedient to what the Lord advises. Secondly, Jesus had already said, "Let down the nets for a draught," but Simon was disobedient and insisted that he would let down a single net instead. We see how clearly doing things we feel is best instead of listening to the Lord is very unwise. In this instance there was such a multitude of fish in the single net that it broke. Worse still, the boat began to sink. We do well to think how God has given us wisdom, guidance and intellect in Isaiah Chapter 55 from verse 8: "For My thoughts are not your thoughts, neither are your ways my ways, saith the Lord. For as the heavens are higher than the earth, so are my ways higher than your ways, and my thoughts than your thoughts." His way is best.

That night as I read the entire Gospel of Luke, I felt I had been given a very special honour of learning how God delights to answer every individual prayer in His own unique way. However, I was in for a further treat. He promised to teach me how to pray effectively. To pray in the way He wants to hear rather than simply listening to my casual chat. There are very valuable lessons and rewards to be gained if we approach His throne with the right attitude and with great expectations. Dare to be a Daniel. Expect great things from a Great God!

Six

Within just a few weeks following my conversion I knew that I would be called up for National Service. I was seventeen years of age.

With my special God-given gift for reading and writing I wanted somehow to expand this in military service. I prayerfully decided to go to the Recruitment Office in Oxford to discover what was on offer.

I was given options of either the Army or the Royal Air Force. There were so many opportunities on offer, but I realised I had no qualifications or examination success for any of them.

I only had two and a half years working at the International Stores grocery shop at Wantage. How could I relate that to wanting to write and get better educated? Then a brochure took my eye.

The Royal Air Force was advertising for provisioning clerks. I thought such a job would be ideal for me. After all, I wanted to write and I was working in a shop which was provisioning on a daily basis. I assumed that the RAF would want someone like me to do some sort of shopping lists. I expected to be provisioning for tea, coffee, sugar, bacon and everything connected to the kitchens and feeding the airmen.

The recruiting officer warned me that I could not be considered for the RAF in that particular trade. The minimum requirement for me was to serve an extra year to make a total of three years on a Regular Engagement. I volunteered to serve the extra time. I prayed so much that I would pass the exam and I was so grateful that it turned out to be easy and I was successful.

After initial entry at RAF Halton in Buckinghamshire I was posted for square bashing and training at Padgate near Warrington in Lancashire. Then from Padgate I was transferred on to the provisioning clerk course at Credenhill near Hereford.

Day one on the course came as a very great shock. I discovered that I would not be provisioning for the kitchens at all. A provisioning course in the RAF meant, in my case, provisioning for spare parts and larger items for the aircraft themselves.

I was taught the importance of obtaining all things required on Canberra jets to get them back in the air when they had been grounded for repairs or replacements.

At that time I had never seen a Canberra jet. I knew even less about the parts and the procedures of how to obtain them, record them and despatch them to where they would be required.

There were thirty-two of us on the course. Sixteen to each of two billets and they were a great bunch of mates. I did not understand much from the books about aircraft provisioning, but I listened very hard to my friends to learn as much as I could from them. Above all I started walking alone in the solitary parts of the camp and pray earnestly for the Lord's intervention.

I was immediately led to James Chapter 1 verses 5 and 6: "If any of you lack wisdom, let him ask of God, that giveth to all men liberally, and upbraideth not; and it shall be given him. But let him ask in faith, nothing wavering. For he that wavereth is like a wave of the sea driven with the wind and tossed."

From just a couple of sentences God had spoken four distinctive things. He would answer my prayer liberally, that is, generous and favourably. He would not upbraid me, that is, to criticise or scold me. He had promised to give me according to my prayer, and I would be blessed if I prayed in faith without fearing. We can know that when God agrees to stand with us we cannot fail but, through Him, know victory.

From that night of praying I did so well on the course because of the Lord's help. Our instructor had never had a one hundred per cent pass from the students and he begged us to do well. This was his last class before retirement and he wanted every one of us to pass. I felt the final exam went very well.

A few days later we were all assembled in a large hanger where the instructor gave his report and the results. He was disappointed. He had not got his one hundred per cent pass because just one of us had let him down. I was the only one who had failed.

That night was the most miserable of any I could remember. Thirty-one of the students were all sent home on a couple of weeks' embarkation leave before being posted to 401 Air Stores Park at Eindhoven in Holland. I was left alone in a billet looking at fifteen empty beds and a complete empty billet next door. I lay in bed listening to a thunderstorm, desperately lonely and a failure. All my friends were successful, on holiday and preparing to go on adventures outside Britain.

The authorities designated me to join the kitchen staff until a decision could be made about my future. I was destined to clean out porridge boilers and clean eating areas. I decided that God had let me down.

The devil comes in many forms when we go through trying and testing times. It is not difficult for us to take our eyes off the Lord and look at the situation and circumstances that surround us.

Within a week an officer called to see me with some news which he thought was extraordinary. He had been informed by the Air Ministry to give me private tuition and revision on the provision course I had failed. He had never come across such an arrangement in all of his time in the Service.

The officer set me some assignments and then left me to get on with them. He seldom looked in to see what I was doing because he was leaving the Service. Getting his affairs together was taking priority upon his time.

A couple of weeks later I was allowed to take a similar exam, which I passed with flying colours. Although the RAF was delighted, they could not understand why I had failed the first time. Even in their view, they remarked how remarkable it was that I had been given such unusual treatment and personal teaching.

I was delighted to find myself on two weeks' embarkation leave immediately before finding that I was being posted as a solitary airman to Germany.

I loved Royal Air Force Wildenrath from the first day that I was posted there. On the first day I had a lovely interview with the commanding officer, who introduced me to the work I would be doing. In conversation I mentioned that I only had one little disappointment about the posting and that was because my thirty-one friends had been posted to Eindhoven.

The officer smiled. "I have some good news for you," he said. "The Air Ministry is closing down the camp at Eindhoven and very shortly everyone there at 401 Air Stores Park will be transferred here to 402 Air Stores Park." I could not conceal my joy and the delight of meeting up with my old pals again.

The only difference was that there were changes here at Wildenrath. There were not enough provisioning clerk vacancies available. Some of the trained clerks were put on various other jobs and assignments.

One evening the lad who was in the next bed to mine made a very casual comment. "Hey, Ken!" he exclaimed. "How is it that you were the only one out of thirty-two of us to fail the course? How is it that you got the best job because you arrived at the camp before us?"

You see, God was with me all the time and working His purposes out for my good. In retrospect I see how he held me back to put me ahead of the rest. Is anything too hard for the Lord?

During my last few months in the RAF our unit was sent on a two-week special Tactical Air Force Exercise to Zandvoort in Holland. The whole unit was in tents under camouflage in a very large thick forest of trees. The idea was that we could not be seen from the air but able to cope with all the office work and the storing and delivery of stores to other units in Germany. All this in a different country and under difficult conditions.

The exercise had a twofold purpose. First that we could

function at full speed in tents. Secondly, masses of stores were stored in the backs of a lot of Magirus Deutz lorries adopted for the purpose. We were ordered to work at increased capacity under these unusual circumstances.

I was in charge of three lads and it rained hard every day for almost the fortnight. During the first week I lost two lads. One from an injury and another who was flown home because of the death of a relative.

The third lad was very new and not fully trained on the job. He made so many mistakes with the paperwork. I got well behind because it took such a long time for me to rectify his mistakes. Our officer in charge decided I would be much quicker if left alone and the lad was moved on to another job.

For the last week of the exercise I was glad to get out of the sodden tent. I slept very little and hour after hour produced documents to authorise the issue of aircraft spares from the backs of the lorries. At the end of the exercise our officer said my extra effort had increased the workload by over thirty per cent. God was with me.

To my absolute amazement the station commander invited me to his office some weeks after the exercise. At the meeting I was told that he had recommended me to the air officer Commanding the 2nd Tactical Air Force for a special commendation for meritorious service. The chief would present me with the prestigious award after the annual parade at the Wildenrath Station. The date was the 22nd of April, which was the same day as my twenty-first birthday.

What a wonderful day it was. It was a very special moment to be drawn from the parade ground to meet the chief of the Air Staff and to receive the written commendation. An unforgettable event for my very special birthday. A very special Lord Jesus Who had allowed me to receive a very special "well done!" publicly.

The same friends who more than two years earlier had witnessed my embarrassment at being the only one to fail the course exam before them.

It is easy in retrospect to see how God orders our footsteps in the path of life. He is constantly working for our good, especially when we feel we have failed or get called to endure unhappy circumstances.

We do well to learn from the experiences of Joseph in the Bible who was sold into slavery by his brothers. Joseph was falsely accused of rape and imprisoned. He suffered many things until God's time came for his deliverance and blessing.

God watched over Joseph. He was honoured and promoted to become second to Pharaoh in the land of Egypt. God honours those who honour Him.

Even in prison Joseph was still under the watchful eye of God. Genesis Chapter 39 verse 23 records, "The Lord was with him, and that which he did, the Lord made it to prosper." Joseph himself was also able to testify to the brothers who had treated him so badly. In Genesis Chapter 50 verse 20 he says, "But as for you, you thought evil against me, but God meant it unto good, to bring to pass, as it is this day, to save much people alive."

If God is for us, who can be against us? The Apostle Paul wrote to the Romans in Romans Chapter 8 verses 38 and 39, "For I am persuaded, that neither death, nor life, nor angels, nor principalities, nor powers, nor things present, nor things to come, nor height, nor depth, nor any other creature, shall be able to separate us from the love of God, which is in Christ Jesus the Lord." I can well say "Amen" to that.

SEVEN

I know I have been very privileged to believe that God answers every individual prayer since I was eight years old. Not always in the way I had hoped and sometimes disappointed when I thought He was not interested in what I was asking. The problem was I was asking for so much. In fact, it was not so much as asking but actually telling God what to do and on a daily basis.

Every morning I would commence by giving God His orders for the day. I told Him what I wanted Him to do. I insisted that He should bless this one and that one. I told Him what I needed and gave good justification why. I never ceased to ask for so many blessings for myself. I can be so very selfish! Then when I had given God His instructions for the day, I would remind Him of what I asked for with an added list of requirements.

Early one morning the Lord interrupted my day's business because I could hardly call it praying. I felt He was saying, "Who are you to tell Me, the Lord Almighty and the King of Glory, what to do? Read my instructions in the Word."

St. Matthew Chapter 7 verse 7: "ASK and it shall be given you: seek, and you shall find; knock, and it shall be opened unto you."

St. John Chapter 14 verse 14: Jesus said, "If you shall ASK anything in My Name, I will do it."

St. John Chapter 15 verse 7: "If you abide in Me, and My words abide in you, You shall ASK what you will, and it shall be done unto you."

Finally I felt as though Jesus gave me a smile as He continued from Revelation Chapter 3 verse 19: "As many as I love, I rebuke and chasten: be zealous, therefore, and repent."

I knew I was without excuse and accepted the Lord's rebuke and that He was chastening me for my own good. Out of His perfect love He was showing me that the formula, or the method of achieving something, is not dependant on demanding and giving orders. The perfect answer lies in that one and only very small word: "Ask!"

Watch beleaguered parents Christmas shopping with a small child in tow. When the child continues to harass and demand toys or goodies you see the exasperation on Mum and Dad's faces. How often do you hear them say, "Hush!" "Be quiet," "Stop wanting things!" "Wait!" The child is not doing himself any favours. However, notice the difference on behalf of the parents when the child is orderly and says politely, "Mummy or Daddy, may I have…" The reaction of the guardian is completely different and so is the response. "Alright, dear. Just a moment, we will have a look in a minute." That is far better than all the scolding and achieves more. Sometimes our Heavenly Father has the same attitude in similar circumstances. I learnt early to ask, never demand and always be patient.

For most of my life I have always followed the same pattern for prayer. From the beginning I have modelled my prayers in the way Jesus taught us Himself in the Lord's

Prayer in St. Matthew Chapter 6 commencing at verse 9. I pray thus.

Almighty God, Loving Heavenly Father, I draw near to You in the blessed Name of Jesus. Lord, I come to praise, love and adore You, because You are worthy of all praise and glory.

Lord, I do give thanks for all Your mercies and blessings and to give thanks for all that You are doing for me and for all your blessed answers to my prayers.

Dear Father, I come now to confess that I have sinned against Heaven and in Your sight and I am not worthy to be called Your Servant. Father, please forgive me for all my sins and my unrighteouness and for all that I have done to grieve You.

Father, I confess… and there I pour out my sins and things I feel it is necessary for me to confess. Then after my confession I pray, "Loving Father, please forgive me for all of these my sins, and for all sins that I am not even aware of. Please, Father, forgive me and cleanse me from all sins and unrighteousness through your Precious Blood. Thank You, Loving Father, for all Your mercies and for restoring me to Your loving fellowship. I love You. Amen."

At this point I thank God for all the answers to prayer and tell Him how much I appreciate various things He has done for me. I consider this vitally important before asking (not telling or dictating) what I wish God to consider. The Apostle Paul made this very clear when he wrote to the saints at Philippi. Philippians Chapter 4 verse 6: "Be careful for nothing; but in every thing by prayer and supplication with thanksgiving let your requests be made known unto God."

It is so easy to fall into the trap that nine of the ten lepers fell in after they had all been healed. Only one returned to thank Jesus for healing them. In St. Luke Chapter 17 Jesus not only noticed this fact (He knoweth all things) but He remarked, "Were there not ten cleansed? but where are the nine? There are not found that returned to give glory to God, save this stranger."

It has well been said, "A little appreciation goes a long way."

Another valuable secret that I learnt from the Lord is the exercise of faith when we speak to Him. I hear so many negatives because folk pray and do not believe or expect a fruitful answer. Jesus addresses this in St. Mark Chapter 11 verse 24: "Therefore I say unto you, What things so ever you desire, when you pray, believe that you receive them, and you shall have them." Remember that is a promise from the Master Himself. Times without number I have found God knows my thoughts before I have prayed. Isaiah Chapter 65 verse 24: "And it shall come to pass, that before they call, I will answer; and while they are yet speaking, I will hear."

Too many people approach God in prayer but from the outset are doubtful or disbelieving that He will answer. Such folk are timid that God does not understand or that He will automatically disappoint them. We look at people who fail and let us down constantly. In like manner we seem to fit God into that mould. We forget that God Almighty has unlimited *power*. He is omnipresent, present everywhere at the same time. He is omnipotent, having absolute unlimited power, and He is omniscient, knowing everything. Consequently there is no-one like Him and according to Ephesians Chapter 3 verse 20 the Apostle Paul says, "Now unto Him that is able to do exceeding abundantly above all that we ask or think, according to the power that worketh in us."

Note that very important fact. God works exceedingly and abundantly above anything we can ask or imagine. This wonderful fact is because God uses His power to work through us. Imagine that the next time you feel useless or powerless. A centurion in St. Matthew Chapter 8 was concerned that his servant was very ill at home. Jesus offered to go to the home and promised that he would heal him.

Feeling unworthy of taking Jesus home, the centurion said, "Speak a word only, and my servant shall be healed." Now that was faith. The centurion acknowledged that Jesus needed only to say a word and his servant would be healed from afar. That is the type of faith Jesus is interested in and rewards accordingly. Jesus spoke concerning the centurion's faith and reminds us with His words, "I have not found so great faith, no, not in Israel." Faith and belief in what Jesus would do was rewarded because the servant "was healed in the selfsame hour".

I rejoice at the way God has done many such miracles in my own experience. In St. Mark Chapter 9 verse 23 Jesus says, "If you can believe, all things are possible to him that believeth." Belief is the key that opens the door of access to God. Unbelief ties up His hands as we read in St. Matthew Chapter 13 verse 58: "And He did not many mighty works there because of their unbelief."

Eight

Wherever we look in the Bible we read about people who had faith in the Lord. Their faith was greatly honoured by God so that they were mightily blessed and used by Him. The writer to the Hebrews in Chapter 11 records several of them and recommends them for what they accomplished or witnessed because of their faith. Hebrews Chapter 11 reminds us, "Now faith is the substance of things hoped for, the evidence of things not seen. For by it the elders obtained a good report. Through faith we understand that the worlds were framed by the word of God, so that things which are seen were not made of things which do appear."

Jesus Himself spoke to Thomas of his unbelief. The other disciples had spoken to him of the fact that they had seen Jesus after he had risen from the dead. Thomas did not believe any one of them and wanted evidence.

In St. John Chapter 20 verse 29: "Jesus said unto him, Thomas, because you have seen me, you have believed, blessed are they that have not seen, and yet have believed."

I can understand how Jesus must have been disappointed at being disbelieved or suggesting a lie had been told. It often happens to me and when the confrontation comes from other Christians it can be very hard to accept.

I share a couple of incidents.

I had the joy of marrying a very special famous celebrity to his partner several years ago. The wedding was at 2pm. I arrived at the church an hour before the wedding and went in via a back door to avoid the press outside and to meet the bridegroom. The bride arrived early for the wedding and we had such a wonderful, unforgettable, happy day.

The following day no two daily newspapers ran the same story. Some papers said the bride arrived from ten minutes to more than half an hour late. Several Christians confronted me days later to suggest the bride appeared to be reluctant to get married.

Every time I explained that the bride was very early for the wedding I was disbelieved. I was surprised and a little hurt that so many said, "We know she was late because we read it in the newspapers." Why was it that my Christian brothers and sisters were more ready to read accounts in the newspapers when I was there and a witness?

I remember an incident in late 1993 whilst watching the television news. The newscaster reported that a young Luton Town footballer called Darren Salton had been injured in a car crash. Darren was on a life-support machine in Addenbrookes Hospital, with his parents and girlfriend being at his bedside. There was little hope of Darren recovering and his condition was deteriorating more each day.

Now I had never heard of Darren Salton and to be honest I am not very interested in football. Normally I would not give that bit of news a second thought.

All evening following the news programme I could not get Darren off my mind. The late news retold the story and the manager of Luton Town spoke of his anguish about the accident and the loss of such a fantastic player. Further news revealed that Darren's life was nearing its end.

When I went to bed I felt the Lord urging me to speak to Him about Darren. The Lord gave a picture in my head concerning him, his parents and a younger brother and his girlfriend. I could see them all so clearly and observed how heartbroken they all were. I knew I was on holy ground when the Lord spoke into my heart, "I am the resurrection and the life," and I felt impelled to carrying on praying until God gave me His assurance from the story of Lazarus in St. John Chapter 11 verse 4: "This sickness is not unto death, but for the glory of God, that the Son of God might be glorified thereby." I knew instantly that God had got everything under control concerning Darren and that He wanted to speak to the family through me.

I have no idea why God sometimes brings to my attention complete strangers, their needs, and urges me to be His servant in these instances, but it happens very often. Neither do I always understand why or how God gives me absolute assurance that He is going to do something special and confirms it by showing me different places in Scripture.

Finally He gives me such conviction of what He is doing that there is no doubt at all. When He does this I can speak with absolute assurance especially after the Lord has confirmed in my mind several times what He has prepared. I believe in proving all things according to Ephesians Chapter 5 verse 10: "Proving what is acceptable unto the Lord." I am able to speak with confidence and exercise all faith in the Lord but only when He has made it so abundantly clear to me in several ways. Without that direction, guidance and assurance, I could never move a step. I am so mindful of Psalm 19 verse

13: "Keep back Thy servant also from presumptuous sins; let them not have dominion over me: then shall I be upright, and I shall be innocent from the great transgression."

In Darren's case I was excited to contact his family and girlfriend to share with them the good news of what God was going to do. How could I tell them that? "This sickness is not unto death, but for the glory of God." We had never met and we did not know each other. The only contact I could make was by writing to the family at the bedside at the hospital and I decided to send them a book I had written about miracles years earlier. I did just that supported with more prayer.

A week later Darren's father telephoned me to thank me for the book and letter. They were so appreciative of my prayers but there was very little hope and Darren was not so well. I promised to leave it with the Lord and asked them to thank Him when Darren was better. Then there was continuing silence and no further reports in the newspapers.

At this juncture I was attacked from Christians on many sides. I was challenged and attacked from many quarters and told that I was irresponsible and the giver of false hope. "Why," they asked, "did you give them such assurance? What if he dies? Why have you given them false hope? After filling them with so much hope how will you deal with the bereavement? How will the family think about Jesus when it doesn't work out? Don't you think you have let the Lord down?" On and on the criticism went, so I had obviously wasted my breath about all that the Lord had shared with me. I was glad that they were not called to interceed. I could only say what Jesus said: "This sickness is not unto death, but for the glory of God." if They could not accept or believe it that was not my fault.

I have always wondered why whenever the Lord gives me some amazing revelation; nearly always it is Christians who disbelieve and endeavour to pour cold water on my enthusiasm. I find very often that non-Christians get more excited about hearing of miracles. Sometimes it seems to be that some Christmas act as though they want to triumph over failure. It is a terrible thing to gloat and say, "I told you so." It is hardly the Lord's way.

Christmas Eve that year I had an evening telephone call from Darren's father, John, enquiring how I was. Moreso I was eager to ask him for news of Darren. John said simply, "Someone wants to speak to you," and handed over the telephone.

"Hello, Ken, it's Darren," the voice said. I wept with joy at the conversation that followed. Darren was so very much better and in recovery had been sent home. I was invited to fly to Edinburgh to meet all the family and Darren invited me to his wedding to his girlfriend the following year. Darren's amazing recovery and the events that followed just proved even greater miracles were in store.

At Darren and Sarah's wedding I shared with friends how the Luton Town Football Club manager's television newscast had prompted me to pray in the first place. I learnt that although Darren would not be playing professional football because of leg injuries, it would not be possible for financial purposes to keep him on the books. The Lord had already assured me about this even before the wedding, so I made it known that if Luton Town would honour commitments to Darren, God would honour the club, and at the end of the season the team would play at Wembley. How individuals laughed and pulled my leg. "That would be a miracle," some said.

Others spoke about past form and enquired, how much did I know about football?

"Not much," I admitted, "but I do believe in a God Who keeps His promises and performs miracles."

God loves to answer prayer and He is never a disappointment, and so I prayed for Luton Town Football Club through the rest of the season. I wanted to see some replays to bring in extra gates and finance. Of course, God never failed.

Luton beat Southend 1-0. Luton then drew with Newcastle United 1-1 and so that called for a replay and another crowd when the next score was 2-0 to Luton. The next match was a 2-1 victory for Luton over Cardiff City. The next match was between Luton and West Ham United, when the score was 0-0, and fortunately for Luton another crowd and another replay. In the closing part of the replay Luton beat West Ham 3-2 at almost the very end of the game. This was an amazing result and that year the Football Association decided the semi-final would be held at Wembley. Luton Town was matched to play Chelsea on 9th April 1994.

Luton Town gave me two tickets to the semi-final and I took a young friend with me. We watched the team come out to the Wembley turf accompanied by Darren as a spectator. We saw the dark overcast sky suddenly became light as a single shaft of sunlight fell down where Darren stood. I felt my eyes sting with tears as I saw Darren seemingly illuminated. I sensed the Lord saying, "I honour them that honour Me."

When the match ended one of the first people that we met inside the stadium was Darren himself. It was such an emotional meeting and not one little bit disappointing that on this occasion Luton lost. God is never a disappointment.

There had been a lot of leg-pulling at Darren and Sarah's wedding when I prophecied that God had said He would bless Luton Town Football Club. He had promised to prosper the matches, bring in the extra finances and give the club the honour of playing at Wembley. God undertook in every single detail.

Even in spite of the fact that God had made His will known and carried out His promises in every possible way, I was astounded that some of my Christian brothers and sisters said I was lucky! What rubbish. I do not believe in luck and superstition, but with God I do acknowledge never-ending amazing divine appointments.

NINE

Without exception everybody enjoys receiving a gift. It may be a birthday or a Christmas gift. Sometimes the urge comes to bestow some special present on someone they love or truly appreciate. I know from experience that God delights in showering us with such gifts every day of our lives.

In St. Matthew Chapter 7 verse 11 Jesus said, "If you then, being evil, know how to give good gifts unto your children, how much more shall your Father which is in heaven give good things to them that ask Him?"

Thinking back on my life I have been pondering on some of the very special gifts God has given me. Not that I deserve any one of them but He is faithful and it causes me to reflect on so many of them recorded in Psalm 103. A gentle reminder of verse 2: "Bless the Lord, O my soul, and forget not all His benefits."

I am persuaded that the gifts that God has given me I have been able to use every one. Not only in thanksgiving and praise for all He has given, but the fact that I am able to use those gifts in His Service.

I have found in life that many individuals have not really realised or accepted each God-given gift they have received.

Consequently they have missed out on so much blessing and guidance that they could enjoy. Even the Apostle Paul, writing to young Timothy in Timothy Chapter 1 verses 5 and 6, said, "Wherefore I call to remembrance the unfeigned faith that is in you... Wherefore I put you in remembrance that you stir up the gift of God, which is in you." Maybe God is reminding us of this today. After all, we must accept the gift before we can use it. I am so thankful that God gave me the gift to read and write. As a very young Christian this gift was to be a twofold blessing in my own experience. First that I was able to read God's words to me through Scripture. Secondly I felt that He was encouraging me to copy out in longhand writing the entire sixty-six books of the Bible. I recognised that this would cause me to concentrate on what the Bible teaches and give me the experience of actual writing. I was excited with the idea, as I promised God that by His grace, I would undertake this massive task.

With high hopes and expectations I wrote Genesis Chapter 1 on the first page of A4 lined paper. I got some way into the book when I realised I had taken on more than I could manage. If my time of copying out the Bible was unrestricted all would be well, but at this time in my life, I was preoccupied with many things.

Apart from my secular job with the Ministry of Defence I was caring for a disabled mother at home. I had become a leader of a Christian youth club in another village and taken on the pastorate of a non-conformist church in a further village. All in all, every day was extremely busy, which left me little time for copying out the entire Bible in longhand writing.

I agonised over the fact that prayerfully I had promised

God that I would copy out the entire Bible. I soon discovered this was not feasible and too time-consuming. I could not spend so much time writing and at the same time serve the Lord and cope with my secular job and private life at the same time. So what about that promise I made to God? I took the whole matter to Him in prayer.

That day I received a valuable lesson from Deuteronomy Chapter 23 verse 21: "When you shall vow a vow unto the Lord your God, you shall not slack to pay it: for the Lord your God will surely require it of you, and it will be a sin in you." Then in my daily Bible readings in the very same week I was led to read Ecclesiastes 5 verse 4: "When you vow a vow unto God, defer not to pay it; for He has no pleasure in fools; pay that which you have vowed. Better it is that you should not vow, than that you should vow and not pay (perform)!"

From that day I have always tried extra hard not to make promises that I will not or intend to keep. From experience I have found this is a grave failure in Christians. It is unbecoming of servants of the Lord. I have lost count of the numerous times I have been promised appointments, ministry engagements, donations or help and then nothing. It happens all the time. It does not bother me personally because God never fails to make everything up to me from His other resources. It does, however, make me sad that He is under-valued. Jesus says, "Inasmuch as you have done it unto one of the least of these my brethren, you have done it to Me." The vow effects the Lord the same as it does to me.

With my decision not to copy out all the Bible, I decided to compromise and copy out the entire New Testament instead. Twenty-seven books instead of sixty-six. I hate compromise, but I felt I was doing the best I could.

It took sixteen months for me to copy out the New Testament on 684 pages of A4 paper. This meant writing every single day. Some days a couple of pages or more as I felt led and not restricted by time. Some days I had wished I had not started the project because it was so time-consuming. If on checking I discovered I had spelt a word wrong, caused a blot (it was written by a fountain pen) or missed a word or made a mistake, I would re-write the entire page. Invariably the mistake was on the second side of the sheet and so both pages had to be rewritten so that it had to be perfect for God. Consequently because of the rewritten pages I must have completed a thousand in total. Someone once observed that I appeared to have a good knowledge of the New Testament. I replied it was because I had made so many mistakes and rewrites that it came very committed to memory.

It was a great day when I wrote the last Chapter of Revelation and took it to a binder, who sewed it together between hard covers with the words "NEW TESTAMENT" in gold.

Praying over the book, I felt God was leading me very specifically that I should use it to show and speak to people of His choice. Almost daily Jesus was leading me to St. Matthew Chapter 10 and repeating His direction for my way forward. Verse 18: "And you shall be brought before governors or kings for My sake for a testimony against them and the Gentiles." I knew I had to approach God with my doubtful mind and looking for some assurance. "How can this be?" I asked. "I am no academic. How could it be possible to bring me before kings and governors and world leaders? What could I say to famous men and women with authority and influence?"

The Lord answered my question in the very next verse,

19: "But when they deliver you up, take no thought how or what you shall speak: for it shall be given you in that same hour what you shall speak. For it is not you that speak, but the Spirit of your Father which speaks in you." So I had my answer. I had written the book and the Lord will open the doors that He wants me to walk through. I was called upon to share it with whoever resides inside. I had only to obey and not rehearse what to say because the Lord would speak through me by His Holy Spirit.

To this day I still have the book. The Lord is still continuing to guide me to the ones He wants to speak to. I give God all the glory for the amazing, miraculous occasions that He has arranged. For outstanding conversations, testimonies and unforgettable memories.

The path of life has led me to some of the greatest people and places around the world, including being a resident in thirty-five different countries. Only God in Christ can know the outcome of those private conversations, testimony and the revealing of His will and His word.

I was blessed in two meetings with Her Majesty the Queen when I was able to present her with a handwritten copy of the book of the Proverbs at the first meeting and the Book of Psalms at the second. I was able to present the gospel personally to Princess Diana just after Prince William was one year old. I promised her that I would write a Gospel for him and she was deeply touched by the thought. In due time Prince William and Prince Harry deeply appreciated handwritten copies of the Scriptures, similar to the original New Testament.

Prince Charles was overjoyed with a special Book of Prayers that the Lord led me to produce for him, and Prime

Minister John Major said a similar book of prayers would be treasured by him.

I recall the excitement of being in Washington and visiting the White House for the first time. It was an honour to be a witness to the Presidents Lyndon B. Johnson, Richard Nixon, Gerald Ford and Ronald Reagan during their times in office. They were very happy to sign the New Testament.

One of my happiest times was spent with the Duke and Duchess of Windsor in London. I learnt from the Duchess that the Duke was in hospital for eye surgery and I promised to pray for him. Praise God, He worked a miracle for the Duke and in appreciation they jointly signed a special royal card for me to include in the book.

God has given me the privilege of meeting very special people with extraordinary stories to tell. I remember Anwar Sadat of Egypt signed the book just prior to being assassinated in 1981. Indira Gandhi was also assassinated and I remember being in her lovely home in New Delhi. A little brass ornament which was given to me as a gift as a reminder of the visit.

Spending some time in Israel and Jordan was a lifetime ambition for me. Seeing the sights and experiencing the atmosphere seemed to bring the Bible to life for me. I had good guides and rejoiced at being in Bethlehem, Nazareth, Jerusalem, Caperneaum and many other interesting places where Jesus walked.

King Hussein of Jordan was very interested in my handwritten copy of the New Testament and was happy that I had been in his country. He fulfilled his promise and signed the book at the Dorchester Hotel in London.

Almost three hundred people from many different walks

of life have held the handwritten Scriptures and listened to what the Holy Spirit has spoken to them. Several heads of state from palaces and castles around the world have entered their signatures in the book. Some people, you may be surprised to hear, have been keen to write in the book like the notorious Kray twins, Archbishop Makarios of Cyprus, Pietro Annigoni the Italian painter and Buzz Aldrin who went to the moon, to mention but a few.

God has given me the unceasing privilege of meeting some of the most interesting people on the planet. He has taken me to some of the most exotic places on earth.

I shall be eternally grateful for all God is doing and how He leads me on in every new and exciting experience. He teaches me something new and valuable through every meeting and circumstance.

I have learnt so much from other people's lives and how God has undertaken in so many different ways. In bereavement, sickness, trials and imprisonments. He remains ever-faithful in all our ways and walks of life. He is the unchanging God. He is the Saviour for sinners, Healer, Comforter, the Mighty God and the Everlasting Father. He is and so much more than a husband for the widow, the father for the orphan and a Friend that sticks closer than a brother.

I do not know whether the Lord has anyone else for me to take the New Testament to. I sometimes wonder when He may say, "Give it now to the Save the Children Fund for whom it was committed to in the first place." I believe He would approve of me giving it to this very worthwhile charity to be auctioned for much-needed funds.

As long as the Lord keeps prompting me to take the book to whoever, or wherever, He wills it, I must be obedient that His will and not my will be done! Jesus reminds us continually, "The disciple is not above his master, nor the servant above his Lord."

Churches and fellowships regularly invite me to take this special New Testament along to speak about it. It creates a lot of interest and questions from congregations. The most frequent question asked is, "Of all the many people that you have met, who has influenced or blessed you the most?"

My standard answer is always the same. The author of the Bible, and His Name is *Jesus*.

TEN

One thing that I am truly grateful for is my inheritance. The Apostle Paul reminded the church at Colosse of their inheritance when he wrote Colossians Chapter 1 verse 12, "Giving thanks unto the Father, which hath made us meet to be partakers of the inheritance of the saints in light." Jesus Himself made us solemn promises. In St. Matthew Chapter 19 and verse 29 He has promised that we shall "inherit everlasting life". In St. Matthew Chapter 25 verse 34 He has instructed us to "inherit the kingdom prepared for you from the foundation of the world".

Much greater than the inheritance promised is the honour and privilege that God has bestowed upon us. The amazing love of a God Who sacrificed His only Son, Jesus, to suffer and to die for our sins on a Cross. When we believe on Jesus, repent of our sins and accept Him as our personal saviour, He becomes our own very special "Heavenly Father". We are born again.

At birth we are born of flesh, but when we are born again we are immediately adopted into God's Own family.

The Bible gives us the assurance of this amazing transaction. Romans Chapter 8: "For as many as are led by the Spirit of God, they are the sons of God, For you have not received the spirit of bondage again to fear, but you have received the Spirit of adoption, whereby we cry, Abba, Father. The Spirit itself bears witness with our spirit, that we are the children of God."

To be a child of God far outweighs any inheritance we receive, but Romans Chapter 8 continues that this is only the small part. The greater gift is: "And if children, then heirs of God, and joint heirs with Christ." What can we say about that? Paul says, "Thanks be unto God for His unspeakable gift," and John writes, "Behold, what manner of love the Father hath bestowed upon us, that we should be called the sons of God."

As I continue in the path of life I constantly remind myself that I am a very special person and so is everyone that belongs to God and is able to call Him Father in truth.

We are adopted children of the King of Kings. This means we are members of a very special Royal Family. As children of a King we are Princes and Princesses of the Blood Royal. We are, therefore, expected to live up to our Royal heritage.

We have God-given gifts of power, authority and privilege.

We are ambassadors for a King in this world where He has placed us. Our Father is exceedingly rich. He owns the cattle on a thousand hills. He put every diamond in every mine. The beauty of it all is that we have access to the King's Presence and resources of Heaven every single time that we pray. So now you know the secret of my continuous joy in knowing Jesus.

We can walk through this world and look it in the face. It is not necessary to be depressed, isolated or feel inferior. We are Royalty for time and eternity.

In knowing such a wonderful Father and Friend I ever

long to walk with Him and be led by His example. For this purpose I systematically read through the Gospels of St. Matthew, Mark, Luke and John on a regular basis and endeavour to take His words to heart. For new readers of the Bible this is the best place to start and become acquainted with Jesus's life and teachings.

Ever since I became a Christian I have always wanted to hear good Bible teachers who preach and teach the Word of God. I am always keen to know about God's plan of salvation, need for repentance and how to walk in the ways of the Lord. I have always wanted to learn as much as possible from Bible teachers concerning judgement, the second coming of Christ, of heaven and hell and prophecy. These important matters are very often neglected to be preached in churches. Likewise, how often are we reminded of the Ten Commandments or three very special commandments of the Lord? First that we must pray for the Jews and the peace of Jerusalem. Pray for the persecuted church and Christian brethren as bound with them, and to pray the Lord to send in labourers to win precious souls for His kingdom in His fields which are white unto harvest but where the labourers are few.

Jesus also urges us to pray for rulers and governments and for all who have rule and authority over us. In short to render unto Caesar things that belong to Caesar and also to render unto God the things that belong to Him. Praise, worship and obedience.

One of the many good speakers who came to preach at our little village evangelical chapel was a Canadian evangelist, Dr. John Wesley White. He was studying at nearby Oxford University at the time and he was also a co-worker with Dr. Billy Graham in London.

It was through the ministry of Dr. Wesley White that I learnt many new truths of the Bible, especially concerning Believer's Baptism.

I was interested at the time, but I did not consider it was necessary for me because I had been Christened as a baby in an Anglican church. I argued that as I had been sprinkled at a font there was no need for me to be baptized by immersion in water, as Dr. Wesley White preached.

The local chapel organised for two young men to be baptized by immersion in the River Thames at Abingdon. Peter and Bob were the two candidates and it was not such a very hot day and the Thames looked very cold.

A lot of people came to watch the baptism and it really was a very joyous and uplifting occasion. The two young men looked radiant as they witnessed for the Lord in the water. It was thrilling to feel the very Presence of God very much in evidence.

Later, at home, I thought about the event and decided I wanted to be baptized. I thought it must be important because Jesus was baptized by immersion and in obedience I wanted to follow His example.

Some friends mocked my decision, but I was persuaded that I was doing the right thing when I studied the Scriptures.

Was Jesus really baptized by immersion? Yes, He was. St. Matthew Chapter 3 verse 16 says, "And Jesus when He was baptized went up straightway out of the water." John the Baptist would not have gone down into the River Jordan if he could have gone anywhere to carry out a sprinkling. St. John Chapter 3 verse 23: "And John also was baptizing in Aenon near to Salim, because there was much water there: and they came, and were baptized."

A further point became crystal clear when I read the account of how Philip baptizsd the eunuch in Acts Chapter 8 verse 36: "And as they went on their way, they came unto a certain water: and the eunuch said, See, here is water; what doth hinder me to be baptized?" In verses 38 and 39: "And they went down both into the water, both Philip and the eunuch; and he baptized him. And when they were come up out of the water, the Spirit of the Lord caught away Philip, and the eunuch saw him no more: and he went on his way rejoicing." No sprinkling but definitely immersion.

Baptism by immersion is a picture of Jesus being buried in death. Rising up from the water is further significant of His resurrection. The Apostle Paul makes this very clear in his letter to the Romans Chapter 6 verses 3 and 4: "Know you not, that so many of us as were baptized into Jesus Christ were baptized into His death? Therefore we are buried with Him by baptism into death: that like Christ was raised up from the dead by the glory of the Father, ever so we also should walk in newness of life."

Arrangements were made for me and another young man to be baptized in a church in Oxford. It was such a joyous occasion for both of us as we went into the baptistery of fairly warm water with Graham Stokes the County Evangelist. The experience was such a blessing and I would not hesitate to recommend Believer's Baptism by immersion for all who are seeking the Lord in this way.

Graham presented me with a beautiful Baptismal Certificate after the event and wrote a text on it from Colossians Chapter 1 verse 19: "For it pleased the Father that in Him should all fulness dwell." A beautiful remembrance too of when the Spirit of God descended upon Jesus at His baptism and when the voice of God spoke to Him from Heaven, saying, "This is my beloved Son, in Whom I am well pleased." I felt that God was pleased that I had been baptized in His Name also.

Eleven

The teaching I had received from Dr. John Wesley White taught me the need to seek God's will and future service. Dr. White often said two things which prompted me to ponder the truth which lay beyond. First was, "We are saved to serve," and also his reminder of Jesus's words: "Other sheep I have, which are not of this fold: them also I must bring."

Many of us are saved, as it were, by the skin of our teeth. We have been born again and know the Scriptures. We go regularly to church and pray. All this is very commendable, but are we concerned for others?

We can have amazing head knowledge of the Bible and memorise and quote texts, chapters and verses. It is commendable to join Christian advances and retreats. We also assemble ourselves for conferences, synods and courses, and train for never-ending fields of service. What is the purpose of it all if we are not producing any results from all the time and energy spent? It is so easy to talk the talk, but God is looking for His children to walk the walk.

James, in his epistle Chapter 1 verse 22, says, "But be you doers of the word, and not hearers only, deceiving yourselves." How often have I heard folk referring to some such individual saying, "He, or she, is too heavenly minded to be of any earthly use."

We shall never win souls for the Lord by much talking or persuasion solely on our part. This must be done prayerfully and carefully working together with God. The Apostle Paul writing in Romans 10 to the church, said, "How shall they call on Him in whom they have not believed? And how shall they believe in Him of Whom they have not heard? And how shall they hear without a preacher? And how shall they preach except they be sent? As it is written, How beautiful are the feet of them that preach the gospel."

Here Paul has outlined the plan in a nutshell. God expects us to go out to others. We are not required to stay at home or in church and simply pray that the Lord will send people to us. He says, "Beautiful are the feet," and this indicates God has given us feet to walk in His ways and to go out to where people are. Jesus's last words before He ascended back to Heaven were words requiring action. "Go you therefore, and teach all nations, baptizing them in the Name of the Father, and of the Son, and of the Holy Ghost: Teaching them to observe all things whatsoever I have commanded you: and, lo, I am with you always, even unto the end of the world."

This serious statement of Jesus comes in the form of a commandment from our King and Heavenly Father, and we do well to consider it.

What seemed to me to be a real answer to prayer was when a young American airman called Master Sergeant Fred Moody, his wife Marilyn and two very young daughters called Diane and Vicki came to live in a small village three miles away from my home. The Moody family were Christians and had been posted to the air base at Brize Norton, but there was not a married quarter available for them. Fred thought this very strange at the time, but the United States Air Force rented them out a civilian house locally which was fifteen miles away from the base but right within my vicinity.

This was all clearly very much in the will of the Lord. I was introduced to the family and I was invited to their home and meals and fellowship. It was absolutely wonderful to meet with these lovely people and they have remained friends and remained in contact to this day.

In those first weeks the Moodys took me to another air base at Upper Heyford, where Fred was invited to preach some Sunday afternoons. Marilyn and the girls would sing together and Fred accompanied them with his guitar. Fred arranged with the base personnel for me to preach, but I was a little bit reluctant at first.

The first time I was invited to preach was at a Baptist chapel in the village of Fyfield which was in a three-mile cycling distance from my home. I spent a long time studying for my sermon, "The Marriage Feast at Cana". I was relieved when there was a small congregation to listen to me. At the end of the service I was so unhappy with the way I had served the Lord. The little group looked bored. I ran out of words to say after ten minutes and I had a further ten minutes to complete my preaching hour.

I well recall saying the same things three times over because I had so much spare time left to fill the allocated hour.

I had started my discourse with the words, "Today I would like to take you through the eye of faith to a wedding ceremony at Cana in Galilee," and outlined the story of Jesus turning water into wine at the feast. At the end of the service and just as I was leaving an elderly gentleman accosted me without a flicker of a smile and said, "When you said you was going to take us to a wedding at Cana, I didn't think you intended to do it three times!" I cycled home in tears, feeling very humiliated and despondent, and decided that I would never preach again. Now that Fred Moody was now asking me to preach at the air base I was reluctant but I did not want to let the Lord down and after much prayer accepted the appointment.

At this time in our relationship I was cycling certain days each week to the Moody home for prayer and to discuss our future ministry.

My first preaching with the Americans went down very well. They enjoyed my testimony as well as the preaching. I knew little village chapels in my area would be blessed with Fred's preaching, and having Marilyn, Diane and Vicki to sing would be an added bonus and a further blessing.

In a few weeks we were travelling over quite a wide area. I cycled the three miles to where the Moodys lived and then the family took me with them in their car to the venues. Then, as far as I was concerned, a catastrophe occurred. The family was allocated a married quarter on the base at Brize Norton and would be moving almost immediately.

This was going to be a problem for me. It was one thing to cycle a six-mile round trip from my home compared to a forty-mile journey to and fro theirs. I made it a very real matter of serious prayer and the Lord answered in an amazing way.

The following Saturday I joined a coach party outing to one of the Youth for Christ gospel rallies at Reading. On the way home we stopped at a fish and chip shop for supper.

Mervyn, a young Christian man, stood behind me in the queue and he tapped me on the shoulder.

"Ken," he began, "as you know I am off to India soon to serve the Lord there and there are several things I cannot take with me. I feel led of the Lord to give you my motorbike. You do a lot of cycling for Him and it would be such a help for you."

I was overjoyed with Mervyn's kindness. It was amazing in the way which the Lord was solving my transport problem and to keep the Moodys and my ministry together. Is anything too hard for the Lord? Certainly not!

Our first night together at Brize Norton was one of praise and thanksgiving for Mervyn, the gift of the motorbike, and the continuance and the way forward for our joint ministry. At midnight my enthusiasm for the newly acquired motorbike was at a low ebb, however, when I left the Moodys in one of the worst thunderstorms I had ever encountered.

Undaunted, however, I tightened the helmet strap and set off for home.

Half an hour later I realised I was hopelessly lost. It was easy to follow the signposts in the daylight, but in the dark and a thunderstorm it was confusing. To make matters worse, I realised the headlights were very dim and I was completely unfamiliar with the area.

I was completely lost. I stopped in a very country road, ran my hand over the rain-splattered headlamps and wondered what I should do?

"Are you lost?" I gasped as a young man stepped out of a gateway and strode to where I was sitting on the bike.

"I certainly am," I replied, and explained how I came to be there and how I was looking for the way home.

"Well, you are almost at Clanfield," the stranger continued. "Go back to the last village of Bampton and take the Buckland road as far as the A420. It is well sign-posted from there and you will know the way."

It was absolutely pouring with rain now and I turned the motorbike around and headed for home by the way the stranger had indicated.

When I got home and went to bed I thanked God for the motorbike and my safe journey home. Only then did the significance of the journey and that stranger at Clanfield hit me. Why did I stop at this particular spot on a twenty-mile route? What was a man doing in a gateway after midnight on such an isolated road? Then I realised that I saw no transport and the young man seemed to be in shirt sleeves and did not appear to be soaked in the storm. I can only believe it was a guardian angel sent from God. I think this every time I read Hebrews Chapter 13 and verse 2: "Be not forgetful to entertain strangers: for thereby some have entertained angels unawares."

The motorbike was a real blessing and allowed me to carry on with the Moodys and a female friend of theirs called Roberta, who was called Bobby for short. In a very short time the Moody family, Bobby and I were bonded together, and we went out to evangelise Oxfordshire and well beyond as a little group of six which called ourselves the "Good News Gospel Team".

It was a sad day when we disbanded a few months later. Fred and the family's time for military service in England was terminated as they were called back to serve in America. The days of the "Good News Gospel Team" had come to an end, but many precious souls were saved and blessed and encouraged for time and eternity.

Now I seemed to be back working solo with the Lord again.

It has well been said that when God closes a door He opens a window! That was just how it happened in my experience.

When I left the Royal Air Force I got a job as a civil servant clerical officer with the Ministry of Defence at Didcot.

I worked with Army personnel and civilians for the Royal Army Ordnance Corps. The job was very similar to the post I held whilst serving as an airman at Wildenrath in Germany. The only difference was I was working with soldiers instead of airmen. In a short time I was also invited to lead a small group of folk in Christian Endeavour meetings one day a week in our dinner break. This was very much encouraged by one of the Army colonels and a very dear civilian friend, also called Ken, who invited me to speak one Sunday at his Baptist church in Faringdon. This was very familiar territory to me because it was only four miles away from Uffington where I once lived and had my first introduction to Jesus through the Sunday school.

Over a few months of regular preaching engagements at the Baptist church I encountered a mother and her daughter who were there in the congregation every time I visited. The mother was called Rene and her daughter was called Joyce.

These two ladies stood out in the congregation. I observed fairly soon that they made notes when I preached and they smiled continually during the message, which they frequently endorsed by saying "Amen" or "Alleluia". I confess that I enjoyed preaching at Faringdon because these ladies obviously loved the Lord and were so encouraging. At the close of one of the meetings Rene came to speak to me. She explained that although they loved to come to morning services at Faringdon, they were members of a little Methodist chapel in a small village called Longcot where they only had evening services. I knew it well because my dad worked on a farm there during one of his many farm labouring jobs. It was in the Vale of the White Horse, still only four miles in a different direction from Uffington.

My new friends invited me home for tea, where I met Rene's husband, Len, and I was promptly encouraged to seek the assistance of the local superintendent minister with a view of training and become a local preacher on the Methodist circuit. Len was already a local preacher and he supervised me when I studied four courses and eventually passed the examination. The family were so keen for me to preach at their chapel.

Now, instead of joining the American Moodys each week, I was visiting the family in Longcot. Len and Rene have been away with the Lord for a few years now, but Rene was over one hundred years old before He called her home.

Joyce remains a very precious Christian friend to this day. In the early days of our coming together the Lord led Joyce to play a very big part in my life, especially as He called us to serve Him in a very special way with two Mission youth clubs about fifteen miles apart.

I guess two thirds of my Christian life has been dedicated to youth work but not just youth in particular. The Lord has led me further on in the path of life to come against young drug addicts, alcoholics, vagrants, homeless and folk considered "hopeless cases".

There are no such hopeless cases with the Lord. The Lord gave me a Mission youth club for "un-clubbables", many of whom had been banned from many other clubs. He also inspired me to write about the experiences in a book called *Road to Nowhere* as we sought to bring these lovely young people to walk on a road "Going Somewhere" with Jesus as their personal friend.

God is still working His purposes out in the Mission youth work and we seek to give Him the praise and glory for it. The future is in His hands and we cannot begin to guess what is in store for us. This we do know: He Who commences work is able to finish it and will yet draw many souls unto Himself from the road to nowhere.

TWELVE

The very well-known evangelist David Watson very kindly wrote this foreword for my first book *Road to Nowhere*:

> *Put together these ingredients: a man who cares about children; who really loves young people trapped by the boredom of an aimless existence; who sticks with them through disappointment, violence, stupidity and danger; who dares to believe in a God Who acts; who sees that God answers specific prayers; and who witness the power of Christ transforming "hopeless cases" – and there you have a very moving story.*
>
> *As he ran his youth clubs, Ken came up against gang warfare, enmity and rivalry, drug trafficking and violence. Surprisingly enough, the scene is not the centre of an industrial city but the heart of rural England.*

It all began in a very surreal way, bathed in the birth of a divine appointment.

Weeks earlier I had been invited to meet Graham Ball, who was a Director of Mission for Christ, a ministry of rural evangelism, at Hastings in Sussex.

I was very impressed with the ministry because it was

concerned and led of God to serve in rural areas. Villages and hamlets are so often overlooked, but millions live in these areas. These souls are just as precious as those in the towns and cities.

I undertook training with Mission for Christ and Graham has been a tremendous mentor and encourager, and still is, for the past fifty years of my life and continuing. The training was very professional and I learnt so much about helping closing churches and chapels due to a lack of leadership and dwindling congregations. Many churches are open for just one hour a week on a Sunday. Hundreds of places of worship have no Sunday schools, youth work or Bible studies. Even more sad is, so many preachers are already despondent, there is a lack of prayer meetings, and very little enthusiasm to go and preach to only six or seven stalwarts in the services. Too often there is a lack of potential or Christians who have lost the vision. The Book of Proverbs Chapter 29 verse 18 reminds us, "Where there is no vision the people perish." What a solemn thought. People perishing because we have not cared, prayed or sought the lost. Jesus Himself bids us, in St. Luke Chapter 14 verse 23, to, "Go out into the highways and hedges, and compel them to come in, that my house may be filled." Sadly the days of compelling are past.

I was very keen for our village evangelical chapel to get acquainted with the work of Mission for Christ. With this in mind I decided to invite the director to come and speak to us.

The leaders at the chapel were very impressed when Graham came with some very clear views and suggestions. Consequently we invited him to return in a month's time to conduct a Gospel Rally in our Village Hall.

One of the lessons we learnt was that very often folk will

want to meet on neutral ground initially rather than to join in a place of worship. I was very excited about the prospect and I wanted to invite unchurched people to the Rally. I prayed and resolved that I would invite at least one hundred people to the event and arranged to get that number of professional invitation cards printed.

I intended to keep advertising and inviting people until every invite had been accepted. Not just popped into letter boxes. This was to be person-to-person evangelism and my aim was to invite all ages.

A day or two prior to the Rally I still had quite a few invitations. I decided to cycle into Abingdon, where previously I had witnessed the two young men being baptized in the River Thames.

I visited the park, football ground and toured the shopping area. I spoke to folk in the marketplace and in the street. Finally I went from pub to pub. A few refused the invitation cards, some laughed, but some were interested. I was so keen to get the very last cards accepted, but at eleven o clock at night I decided I had to call it a day. I was a bit disappointed because I still had five invitations left.

I had seven miles to cycle home but this became a hazard because it was well past lighting-up time and I didn't have any lights on my bike. I felt decidedly insecure as cars flashed past me. I decided to get off the main road and push the bike through a small hamlet called Garford. This would be a diversion to my village, just a little bit longer, but at least it would be much safer. I sang Christian choruses as I pushed my bike. I rode some in the dark and hopped off it every time a car overtook me. Then I had the most startling experience.

As I approached the centre of the hamlet I could just

discern the outline of five young people sitting on a low wall. Instantly I remembered I had exactly five Rally invitations in my pocket. It was now almost midnight and I just knew that this was one of those God-given divine appointments.

I propped my bike up and walked over to where they were sitting. I started off with, "Good evening," and without exception they all stood up. I noticed a couple of them had their hands concealed behind their backs.

"I would like to give each one of you an invitation to a Christian Rally," I began. "I feel I should give you these five invitations because that is exactly the number I have got left." A sudden sigh of relief rippled through the assembled group and they all began chattering at once.

At this point, hands came out from behind backs and in the dark I could just see that some of them were holding handfuls of onions and stalks of Brussels sprouts. "We thought you was a copper," one of the lads explained. "They've been looking out for us 'cos we've been knocking off stuff from the gardens."

"Good gracious," I replied. "Is there nothing else to keep you amused?"

The youngsters were swift to point out a large wooden-type hut with a tin roof. It was on the opposite side of the road which I could just discern the shape in the darkness. "That's our village hall," one of the lads explained. "I have lived here six years and I have never seen it open."

"There is nothing to do here," volunteered another youth. "We haven't even got a pub."

We had a lovely chat that evening. My new-found friends listened well to what I had to say about the forthcoming coming Gospel Rally in my village. They were very happy to receive the invitations. They were very clearly impressed when I told them how God loved them and sent five invitations especially for them. They clearly accepted that God must have had a purpose to take me off my route for home, and to ensure they would be at that very place and time to receive the invitations.

I made what I thought was just a simple remark. "You have got a village hall over there." I nodded in the general direction. "Why don't you get together and have some entertainment in it?"

The oldest lad in the group shocked me with his observation. "If you are so concerned for us, why don't you come here and give us a youth club? We would love something like that."

I was challenged. There was an opportunity to give something in that small community. I could see potential for bringing young people to know the Lord. They seemed so lost.

Verses from the Bible sprang to mind. Zechariah Chapter 2 verse 4: "Run, speak to this young man." Especially the Song of Solomon Chapter 7 verse 11: "Come, my beloved, let us go forth into the field; let us lodge in the villages."

It would have been so easy to get all thrilled and enthusiastic to have an opportunity to meet the needs of those young people. I could have made decisions and made promises on the spot as sadly so many Christians do.

I am frequently surprised how so many Christians have "good ideas" and "make proposals" to do this, that and the other for God. Lots of good intentions and a sense of doing something very good. It may be commendable, but is it always what God wants?

Is it what He intends for you? Sadly so many fall into

the trap of doing what God is not wanting of us. It may be undertaking some project or activity which is contrary to His will. I am convinced that there are so many Christians who are very active in Christian work that they have chosen to do, or be part of, which was never God's plan or intention for them in the first place. I mentioned this to a very well-loved evangelist one day. He confessed to me that he had walked a certain path for a number of years until he realised he was doing what he called God's "second best". He repented and the Lord led him into a very different place and ministry.

This dear man gave me some very friendly advice. "So many Christians get good ideas," he said. "It is usually to start some work or activity, open some enterprise or forge ahead with some plan of one's own choosing. This is followed with earnest prayer that God will honour and bless and prosper what has been decided. This is like putting the cart before the horse. The important thing is to seek the Lord's will in what He requires of us and keep seeking until God makes His purposes plain. Then, when we are obedient to do what He wants us to do, we will not have to keep praying the way forward because He will honour and bless what He is doing through His willing and obedient servants. We remember that His servants are not greater than his Lord. If only Moses had fully understood that when he led the Israelites out of bondage in Egypt and led them through a wilderness. It would not have necessitated a wilderness journey that lasted forty long years."

Now I was faced with a decision about the young people seeking my help for a Christian youth club in Garford. I needed to pray and seek the Lord for His decision.

I shared it with friends. "You know what young people

are!" some mocked. "They will not come to anything Christian. They will not give it a single thought. Don't raise your hopes." I often wonder why there is so much negative thought? Through the decades of my Christian life most of the discouragements, doubts, obstacles and criticism I have encountered have come from my Christian brothers and sisters.

I saw some smiling and discussing, and some disapproving when the Gospel started and there was not a sign of a single person from Garford. I often find some folk are happy to see failure just to be able to say, "I told you so!", but this night was to be an exception.

A quarter of an hour into the service and I heard a roar of a couple of motorbikes and a car-load of young people filed into the back of the hall. Some were dressed in leather gear and jeans, some smoking and most of them grinning. What a wonderful sight to see them.

They chatted through some of the service but gathered around me at the end of it. One of the motorcyclists, a big swarthy fellow called Steve, introduced me to the gang, which included a couple of the lads and one of the girls I had met previously.

We chatted about a proposed meeting I should have with the chairmen of Garford parish committee. I had no idea who he was or how his committee would react to me coming into his domain to lead a Christian youth club. I didn't even know what the village hall was like or what facilities were on offer. I promised the little group I would contact them again, and with a cheer they roared off into the night.

A couple of days later I duly arrived at a lovely farmhouse in the village and a very pleasant but amused farmer answered the door.

"Are you the chairman of the parish committee?" I asked.

The farmer laughed. "I am the committee," he replied. "There are not many of us around here and I generally do the business of the village myself."

He never stopped laughing and said he admired my spirit and enthusiasm. "We have tried things here for the youth," he explained, "but nothing takes off here."

I listened to all that the farmer had to say.

The hall had not been used for a very long time. There was no water laid on to the building and only a toilet bucket in a little shed some distance from the building. If used I would have to be responsible for emptying it after each session of the club.

There was no central heating. If I wanted warmth in the winter, I would have to provide my own wood and coal and light a large fire in the old large fireplace. There were no funds available and no games or equipment for the youth to use.

The electricity supply had been cut off months earlier because the hall was not used. The farmer's name was Cliff and he was a really lovely man and could not have been more helpful.

"I am really grateful for your offer of help," he continued. "I will arrange for the electricity supply to be re-connected. I wish you well, but I don't expect you to last here a month." I enquired how much I would have to pay to hire the hall if I undertook two evenings of youth work each week? His final remark filled me with joy and my reply caused him to double up in laughter.

"I will give you my own personal donation for your work. For whatever length of time you use the hall for the young people, you can have it for free."

As I thanked this dear man for all of his valuable help and generosity, I asked him if I could have his agreement for continuous use of the building for free in writing! He very willingly agreed. So I thought I was off to a good start.

Thirteen

I had many misgivings when I called on Farmer Cliff the night I called to collect the key for Garford village hall. I had previously arranged to collect the key from him every time I visited, then to pop it through his letter box every evening when I went home.

Several of the youth were looking out for me and joined me on the trek to the hall. The sight that met us when we got inside was horrendous.

The remains of the last jumble sale littered the floor, ashes filled the grate and cobwebs were everywhere. The windows were filthy and full of dead flies. Thick layers of dust lay on everything, and the smell of damp, mildew and soot was overpowering.

I looked at the little stone-built shed which housed the outside lavatory with its ominous bucket that I had inherited. Inside the hall there was no kitchen or any facilities. I began to wonder how on earth it would be possible to serve drinks or refreshments, or clean or wash anything because water had never been installed. The building started to be built in 1899 to commemorate the commencement of the twentieth century and it was completed the following year. No modernisation had happened since then.

I stepped up on to the old wooden stage which had been used for concerts in days past, but the little group of youngsters looking at me now were looking very forlorn.

"No," I thought, "I just cannot work in a place like this, and that is final."

A lad started rummaging through the remains of the jumble sale at that precise moment. He pounced on an object and jumped onto the stage to give it to me. "Here is summat for you," he said, thrusting a framed but faded watercolour painting into my hand.

My eyes filled with tears. I gazed down at the picture which the lad had just handed to me. I was looking at a most beautiful picture of Jesus that I had ever seen. He was standing in the centre of the picture with His hands spread out above the heads of many youngsters. Underneath the picture in letters of gold and blue I read the caption: "Behold I send you forth."

Ever since that day I have often referred to that breathtaking experience. It was just as though at that moment God had sent me a telegram.

As I started to form the words to say, "No, I cannot work here," I heard myself saying, "Come on, guys, let's start and get the place cleaned up."

I was really impressed with the enthusiasm of the young people as they set to work. Most of them went home to their cottages in the one main street to collect dustpans and brushes, dusters and brooms. A lady opposite came in to see what progress was being made. What a joy when she brought a bucket full of water with her. Later that evening the hall looked very sparse but looking so very much cleaner.

I gave myself a week to obtain essential things for the

club and left them with a promise that we would meet the following Thursday evening. I had seven days to get the most urgent things, but I remembered God created the world in six days, so Him working with us was no competition. What a lot of prayers I offered every day of that week.

I was given an old three-piece suite and some threadbare armchairs. Half a dozen wooden chairs and a couple of plastic ones.

I was embarrassed whilst cycling the three miles to Garford because of all that I was carrying on the cross bar, the carrier and the handlebars on my bike. I looked like a rag-and-bone merchant. I had a two-gallon can of water between me and the handlebars, with carrier bags dangling precariously from both. These contained an electric kettle, tea, coffee and milk. On the carrier I had half a sack of coal and blocks of wood for the fire. I reasoned that if they had something to sit on they could enjoy sitting by a nice fire and enjoy a hot drink. The first night of the Garford Mission Youth Club was launched with a dozen youngsters present.

It was a happy little bunch that sat around the large coal fire drinking tea and coffee and just chatting. From the very first evening I emphasised that we would have a short Bible reading, epilogue and prayer before we went home. They listened well and thanked me profusely for a good evening. One of the lads and a girl hung back to chat further as the others left. "How much will we have to pay to come to the youth club?" they asked. "Will we have refreshments and what will it cost?" They were clearly concerned that there would be expenditure. I told them that I would work it out for the next session.

Now alone, I sat by the large fire with my Bible still on

my lap. As I prayed and thanked God for our meeting, I also asked Him for guidance for the way forward, and what was I to charge and do to cover the expenses. It was at that point that my Bible fell off my lap and hit the hearth and it fell open. As I picked it up I was at Isaiah Chapter 55 and the first verse seemed to leap at me from the page. I read, "Come, buy, and eat; yes, come, buy wine and milk without money and without price." I knew God had answered my prayer instantly. I would tell the youth that there would never be a charge.

Although I do believe that taking responsibility should be taught and folk should not expect everything for free. To this end I put a money box on the mantlepiece at the youth club with the words, "Freewill offerings helps to pay for the refreshments."

More than a hundred youth attended the mission youth club during its nineteen years' existence. The members would drop coins into the money box at every session. They were never asked. I never beg. I just share all my needs with my abundantly rich Heavenly Father. I never see His cheque book, but He sends me cheques from time to time. The Account is in Heaven. The wording on the cheque is Colossians Chapter 4 verse 19: "God shall supply all your need according to His riches in glory." The signature must be Christ Jesus.

Not to boast, but before God and in praise of His Holy Name, I can say I never once had a single bill I could not pay. During the years I was given three minibuses for conveying the young people from a ten-mile radius for the club and ministry around various churches. The tax and insurance for the vehicles was always supplied as well as the wood and coal and refreshments and everything we ever needed at the village hall.

We were, of course, so grateful for the farmer who kept his promise of allowing the hire of the hall to be free over all the years.

It was a very valuable lesson that I learnt the first night of the Garford Mission Youth Club. I realised when God gave me the word, "Come, buy, without money and without price," it was not restricted to the club only but to whatever He called on me to do. The ministry throughout my life has always been trusting in the goodness of God. I have always adhered very strongly to this principle. I have never charged for conducting baptisms, weddings or funerals, although there have been a good many of them. I reckon that I have been given about fifteen cars, maybe more, for the Master's journeys. I have flown twice around the world on ministry and the Lord provided every penny. I constantly experience the promise of Psalm 84 verse 11: "No good thing will He withold from them that walk uprightly."

If I stood outside Buckingham Palace as one of Her Majesty's servants, I am confident that she would not expect me to beg or tout for assistance in order for her work to continue. I am even more confident that the King of Glory would not expect me to beg for Him. Psalm 37 verse 25: "I have been young, and now am old: yet have I not seen the righteous forsaken, nor his seed begging bread."

During the second week of the opening of the club a reporter from a local newspaper came to take some photographs and wrote a glowing report. Consequently several readers sent donations and I was given a table-tennis table which was quickly followed by an almost-new snooker table, cues and snooker balls. Our young people were delighted and twice weekly enjoyed a lot of indoor activities.

Family and friends donated crockery and cutlery and cooking utensils. They also provided a dart board and darts and various games. I bought a double electric ring and a couple of saucepans. We were now well up and running.

Behind the stage was a fair-sized room which was divided by a wooden wall to form two smaller rooms. Two small flights of wooden steps connected the stage and led down to the back rooms. Initially the rooms were designed to be male and female changing rooms when concerts had been staged at the turn of the century. Now I used one of the little rooms as a kitchen where we made drinks and cooked beans on toast, eggs and bacon, or sandwiches, cakes and biscuits. I stored the wood and coal for the fireplace in the second little room.

As the weeks passed the membership of the mission youth club increased. I was welcoming youth from several villages in the district. Word soon got around that we had a very homely club. The large wood and coal fires were a great draw, whilst the young people sat by, eating whatever we provided. Toast, various hot and cold drinks, sandwiches, cakes and biscuits, and a warm welcome. It was all available as each member came in and scanned the day's menu.

Most weekends I continued to visit, and sometimes preach, at Longcot, where I helped at the Methodist church with Rene and Len and their daughter Joyce. This lovely family were so concerned that I was travelling further and further on ministry on my old bicycle. Having experienced a nasty accident on a motorcycle, which resulted in a plastic surgery operation on my face, I decided it was time I sought alternative transport when God stepped in to my rescue.

Len decided to buy another car and very kindly offered me his old one as a gift. I had passed my driving test on a three-ton Magirus Deutz lorry when I was stationed with the RAF in Germany but this only authorised me to drive in the British zone of the country. It was necessary for me to take a British driving test when I came home.

When Len gave me the car, Joyce very kindly volunteered to give me lessons and soon I was in possession of a full British Driving Licence and very much more mobile for going on the ministry. What a blessing it was to be able to convey all the wood and coal, and water and whatever was needed, for the mission youth club at Garford. God looks after all our needs and constantly reminds me what I was taught at Sunday school. "Remember, children, God answers every prayer. Some with 'yes', some with 'no' and some with 'wait'. What He decides is always best."

Fourteen

I remember the first Christmas at the Garford Mission Youth Club for probably not all the best reasons. The youth were very willing to help arrange a party at the village hall and most of them came up with suggestions. Finally we agreed that we would have all sorts of food but only hot and cold drinks but no alcohol.

One of the older lads, called Freddie, was extremely tall and muscular. He had a reputation for getting angry easily and was no stranger to getting into fights with anyone who opposed him. I realised early on that he was ideal to be my youth chairman.

The members were careful not to antagonise Freddie and heeded whatever he said. I know he was God's choice because he was so happy that I had made him responsible for several matters.

Like Job in the Old Testament I have always had my "comforters" who have questioned my plans and poured scorn on my decisions. Experience shows that very often someone who is constantly ignored, ridiculed or undervalued remains despondent, discouraged and feeling worthless. However, when someone realises the good and potential of an individual he invariably responds well and is an asset in the work. Freddie was an ideal choice. He was such a great example and a marvellous help in so many ways.

Imaginative, reliable and constantly loyal. I relied on him so much and he was constantly thanking me for giving him responsibility. It made him feel good. I was deeply saddened when such a faithful friend died fairly young.

There was no shortage of recommendations for the Christmas party and everyone was given at least one task to undertake. In this way everyone plays a part and no-one feels unwanted or left out.

All through the years of the Garford Mission Youth Club there were so many miracles, tragedies, laughter and tears. There were so many adventures and amazing things that happened until one day the young people urged me to write a book about it all. As a joke I agreed and started chapter one, which I read to the assembled club at the next meeting. They insisted on hearing the next chapter the following week, and subsequent weeks, and they got excited to hear about themselves as I changed their names but not the facts. I just did not want to disappoint them and sometimes I wrote the current chapter the night before the meeting. Consequently the book contained forty chapters and was written in forty weeks.

The first Christmas party was a huge success and our young people were encouraged to invite their friends. There was so much fun and happy laughter. It was a tremendous success.

Prior to the party one of the lads arrived with several yards of electric wire, sockets and masses of coloured bulbs which his uncle had loaned for decorating inside and outside the hall. It was a very impressive and grand display and made the little hamlet look like the Blackpool illuminations.

One evening a villager stood outside the hall looking in bewilderment as I switched on the illuminations. "Cor blimey!" he exclaimed. "I can't believe it." This from a villager who'd criticised when we formed the club several weeks earlier. I enjoyed the moment.

"Yes," I added, "the young people have worked hard. It just shows how their hearts are in the right place."

"Yes, their hearts may be in the right place," the local continued, "but this lot" – he nodded at the illuminations – "are definitely not. I am the foreman in my job and I can see that all this have been nicked from where I work."

I was aghast that my very keen helper had not borrowed the lights from his supposed uncle but had purloined them from his employer. I could only stammer out my apologies and promised to return them as soon as possible. The foreman said his employer had not said anything and that he would keep our secret. He also promised in due course to smuggle the lights back from whence they came.

A fortnight later a very well-to-do businessman stopped to chat to me as I was locking the car outside the hall. He introduced himself and with a chuckle said, "I am glad that you found my lights so useful and you had a nice Christmas. If you need any help or ever want to borrow the lights again, just let me know." Off he went with a cheery wave, leaving me with a face as red as the lights themselves. I used Numbers Chapter 32 verse 23 as my text at the next club epilogue session: "Be sure your sin will find you out."

Sometimes whilst working within the club I was not always aware of what was going on outside. All of a sudden I was aware that there were several people outside in the street waving torches in the darkness. I heard a lot of chattering, so I went out to see what was happening.

There was such a lot of laughter and the chatter got louder.

A very lovely European lady lived a short distance from the club with her family, including a daughter who was a member of our club. I will call the mother Heidi because I cannot remember her name.

A group of our lads had got a ladder and leaned it against Heidi's roof, aided and abetted by the daughter. I came out to see one lad clad in a Father Christmas suit heading for the chimney. A fair crowd was gathering and urging him to go on whilst other lads steadied the base of the ladder. It was pandemonium.

Heidi came out into the garden and could not believe her eyes. There was Father Christmas beside her chimney. With arms folded she was speechless for some moments when the lads ran off with the ladder, leaving him stranded on the roof.

"You, naughty boy!" Heidi yelled. "You come down. You will fall. What are you doing?"

"I can't come down your chimney," Santa shouted. "You've got a fire!"

"You stupid boy," she yelled, "you will fall down!" Then, turning to the lads who had run off with the ladder, she shouted, "Bring that back. Now!"

It was at least thirty minutes before we could persuade the lads to return the ladder and we all held our breath as by now the lad had become terrified at the chimney. Very slowly he returned to terra firma when the ladder was raised. Heidi relaxed when she saw Santa was alright, but I could see that she was very much enjoying the attention.

I had another encounter with Heidi very soon after the Father Christmas saga. Heidi very kindly invited me to her mother's one hundredth birthday party at the home. On the day, I travelled by bus to the main road outside the village and walked to the home.

As I arrived I saw there were a lot of cars outside and I could hear music and dancing and a lot of merry-making from within. I arrived with a bouquet of flowers and a box of chocolates for the mother's birthday. I was very warmly invited inside and Heidi greeted me with, "Thank you very much for coming to my mamma's birthday!" I asked where she was because I wanted to give her my gifts. "Come and see!" she replied.

I was taken to look at a very large mirror over the fireplace which had a large photograph of a very distinguished lady on it looking down at me. "That is Mother," it was explained. When I asked where she was Heidi said, "Oh no, she is not here. She died when she was eighty-four. She would have been one hundred today." I am confident that God does have a sense of humour. On reflection I remember 1 Corinthians Chapter 9 verse 22: "To the weak became I as weak, that I might gain the weak: I am made all things to all men, that I might by all means save some."

Almost every week one of the youth club members, who was in some sort of trouble or worried, would bring in a friend from another village or town with similar problems.

Invariably the friend was introduced because he or she was needing help. It was always a golden opportunity for me to say how much Jesus loves them and how He is not only a good listener but very willing to be a very present help in times of trouble.

Not too many folk realise that there are just as many youth problems in the rural areas as in our towns and cities. The big, populated areas have endless opportunities and facilities for sports, gymnasiums, nightclubs, pop groups and socialising. There are opportunities to join football and rugby clubs and a variety of pursuits. In little hamlets like our little Garford there was no public transport unless you walked a mile outside the village for it.

The young people would have to cycle some distance to get a haircut or visit a cinema or visit their friends. It is not surprising, therefore, that left with so much time on their hands, the young people get into mischief or dabble with unsavoury things. It was because of this kind of situation I first encountered the five youths sitting on the wall at Garford in the first place. I remembered how the highlight of their day was stealing vegetables from the neighbours' gardens.

Too often churches and Christians give very little thought to the loneliness and boredom of such people. Where there are no places of worship locally, no opportunity of getting alongside people to share our faith, however will the millions living in the rural areas get to hear or know about Jesus and His love and help? The Apostle Paul constantly reminds us in Romans Chapter 10 verses 14 and 15: "How then shall they call on Him in Whom they have not believed? And how shall they believe in Him of Whom they have not heard? And how shall they hear without a preacher? And how shall they preach, except they be sent? As it is written, How beautiful are the feet of them that preach the gospel of peace, and bring glad tidings of good things?"

Through my entire Christian life I have wondered why so many thousands of believers flock to large congregation churches and be content to sit in a crowd, to allow neighbouring rural churches and chapels to close. I am sure that everyone would like to be part of a large gathering and absorb as much teaching, preaching and fellowship as we can. How wonderful to be part of where it is all happening. Is that good for me? Am I enjoying my fellowship? Do I enjoy being identified as I identify? There is a lot of "me" in that context. There is no harm in being part of something big. There is no compulsion, or need to cancel our membership, or to leave our places of worship where we are happy and blessed, but have I no time at all to visit, encourage, support and especially pray for those who are in danger of losing their place of worship and fellowship completely? They are our brothers and sisters. They are parts of Christ's body and I am convinced that God is not happy to see so many amputations.

I found that word soon got around when I had been some particular help to the youth at the club. There is a lot of truth in the saying "birds of a feather flock together" and the youth continued to bring in friends with similar problems of their own for help.

I have lost count of the number of times that parents have confessed to me: "My boy, or girl, will tell you things he or she will never say to me."

Although I am well aware that it is not always easy for young people to speak to any parent on any matter which may be embarrassing or particularly delicate, or may upset them, I often reply, "Have you taken the time to really sit down and listen? I mean listen, without cutting off the conversation by thrusting home your own theories and opinions almost before they have had chance to open their mouth?" In most cases this has not been so! I have also found that it is the same thing with some of our church and youth leaders. It is not surprising, therefore, that a young person will often go to a friend, where they will get a sympathetic hearing. The secret is to be a good and patient listener. I received this timely advice from a lovely Christian pastor when I was young in the faith. He said, "Listen more and speak less until the Lord tells you what to say."

Jesus was the perfect teacher and listener and led by example. How often we read in Scripture concerning Jesus, Who said, "Neither do I condemn you." "Do not judge." "How much more shall your Father which is in Heaven give good things to them that ask Him?" "I will come and heal him." "Believe you that I am able to do this?" "Have you understood all these things?" "Bring him hither to me."

Jesus was sought by many, seeking help in a multitude of ways. He was never too busy to listen or respond. He spoke the truth with love. No-one ever cared or was concerned as much as He was. It is little wonder, therefore, why we have some excellent in advice in James Chapter 1 verse 22: "Be you doers of the word, and not hearers only," and 1 Peter Chapter 2 verse 21: "Christ also suffered for us, leaving us an example, that you (we) should follow in his steps."

In the first four years of serving the Lord in the Garford Mission Youth Club, I could never have imagined what God had in store, or what He was going to do in the fifteen years which were to follow. I knew that since He had called me to His Service He would fulfil all His promises and guide me. He even confirmed it in writing by leading me to read

Joshua Chapter 1 verse 9: "Have I not commanded you? Be strong and of a good courage; be not afraid, neither be you dismayed: for the Lord your God is with you whithersoever you go." I praise God; He fulfilled it exactly as He promised.

Fifteen

It is a very sad affair when one of your mission youth club members decides to commit suicide. It is even more tragic when he confides his intentions with a couple of friends so that the three of them decide to do it together. The three were in just as much trouble as they could be.

The trio had been drinking and together discussed their problems and decided that life was not worth living. The fact that one of their girlfriends had left for good had not help their melancholy situation either. It was Pat who decided to steal a car and then take his two friends, Del and Barry, with him. It was also Pat's idea to crash the car at speed at a notorious hair-pin bend.

Pat put his plan into action by taking Del and Barry in the car with him. At the crucial bend in the road, the car literally flew through the air and nosedived on its front wheels into a field.

Pat smacked his face against the window and broke his nose. Del was thrown backwards and somehow slipped between the seats so that his body was lying at an awkward angle. He was conscious but complained of an agonising pain, low down in his back. Barry, in the back of the car, was thrown against one of the metal buckles of the seatbelt and was instantly knocked unconscious. The car continued to slide at an alarming speed on the wet grassy field but remained upright.

Pat took over control of the situation and Barry soon came round and was able to help him to try and lift Del from being wedged between the seats. They could not manage to budge Del because of his painful back and now Barry began to feel faint as well. Seconds later, Barry saw a white figure coming towards them and, in his confused state, vaguely thought he was seeing an angel and that he was in heaven. Then darkness engulfed him and he could remember no more.

The next thing Barry knew was that the three of them were in a warm room. The lady in white who was talking to them was not an angel, as Barry envisaged, but a trained nurse who lived almost adjacent to the place where the car crashed.

The nurse telephoned for an ambulance and the lads were mortified when she contacted the police as well to report the accident. Both the ambulance and the police arrived in minutes.

Pat and Barry were taken to a police station for questioning and charged with the car offence and allowed to go home on bail. Del was taken to hospital for investigation on his back but was released the following day. He did not go home but sought out Pat and the two of them went together on a wild spree in Oxford. The pair bought drugs and caused chaos wherever they went. They broke crockery in cafes and during the day Pat hit a traffic warden. Then later on Pat could not even remember stealing a toy gun in a chain store. When he did eventually turn up at home he terrified his parents by holding them up with what they thought was a real gun. Not surprisingly, Pat ended up in prison and awaited the hearing at the Crown Court for stealing and crashing the car, and more recently, for stealing the gun and threatening his family with it.

When Del and Barry's case was heard at the Magistrate's Court they were very heavily fined and both felt they had got off lightly. Pat, on the other hand, appeared before a judge at the Crown Court. To my great concern he was committed to Broadmoor for an unspecified period. I tried to cheer him up by promising that I would visit him regularly, although this would mean a hundred-mile round trip. Pat begged me to take Del and Barry with me whenever I could visit.

Broadmoor Hospital, which seemed to tower above us, resembled a large, red-brick castle, but the thing that struck me most was the quietness of the place. The first visit seemed to pass very quickly with us all speaking at once. Afterwards it took us a further hour to get home, and because we visited on Sundays, I had to take evening services at various chapels in my area during Sunday evenings.

There was no time for tea, but I was deeply touched and impressed when the two lads volunteered to come to the places of worship with me most Sundays.

One afternoon whilst I was driving home down the M4 motorway, Barry made a casual remark which had a long-standing effect on me. Looking at the miles of winding motorway ahead of us he casually said, "Look, Ken, it looks like the road to nowhere." There and then I immediately knew I had the title for the book I was writing, chapter by chapter, week after week, for the members of the mission youth club. It was just that – *Road to Nowhere*.

Every time we visited Pat at Broadmoor he asked me the same question: "How long will I have to stay here?" I promised to seek God in prayer regarding his question.

Each weekday I was still secularly employed with the Ministry of Defence at Bicester. The government provided a coach to convey some of us from this village which dropped us off at a central point. Although there was a connecting coach to drive to our particular offices, I decided to walk the half of a mile for exercise but mostly to pray. The road on which I walked was very high and ran along the side of a hill. I called it the "King's Highway" because it was where I met the King of Kings in prayer every morning. Pat was very much in my prayers at this time and I continued to ask the Lord, "When will Pat be released from Broadmoor?"

I remember it was a Wednesday morning when I was brought to a halt and I felt rooted to the spot on the King's Highway. It was as though the Lord spoke directly into my thoughts and I was aware of an instant answer. It was, "As the leaves so shall the days be."

I looked and saw that I was standing beside a horse-chestnut tree, and on it fluttered a few withered and crinkled brown leaves. I counted twelve only, and without explaining it, I knew inside me that God was giving me the answer. Pat would be released in twelve days. I worked this out that the twelfth day would be a week on Sunday. The day for a visit.

Sure enough, on that very day, it was confirmed that Pat was going to be transferred to another hospital near to home. Then, my prayers were finally answered when I went into the local town a month later and found him talking to a small group of friends outside Woolworth's. Pat was now free and he never got into any trouble again.

God again honoured His word in Isaiah Chapter 59 and verse 1: "Behold, the Lord's hand is not shortened, that it cannot save; neither His ear heavy, that it cannot hear."

Now happily married, Pat remains a very close friend to this day, and he was one of the first visitors to visit me in hospital when I suffered a stroke last year.

I never cease to thank God for so many answers to prayers and miracles that He did for us, during the nineteen years that the Garford Mission Youth Club existed. Glen arrived one evening on his motorbike but explained that he would have to leave early because the lights were not working on the bike and the nights were drawing in. He had been no less than three times to a local garage, but there was something wrong with the wiring. They could not fathom the problem and Glen could not afford another bill.

I saw here was a lesson as I thought of Hebrews Chapter 10 and verses 22 and 23: "Let us draw near with a true heart in full assurance of faith." "Let us hold fast the profession of our faith without wavering: for He is faithful that promised; And let us consider one another to provoke unto love and to good works." Consequently before a group of Glen's mates, I placed my hands on the motorbike headlamps and prayed, and instantly the lights shone brightly all down the road. God spoke to that little group and it was the topic of conversation for weeks because the lights never failed again.

Every week I toured the area driving the minibus, collecting young lads and girls, so that they could come to the club. I saw endless opportunities to witness for the Lord. It served a wonderful purpose for some of those who came were homeless and some had very serious problems.

Some weeks I would pick up lads who squatted in a

disused wooden hut, which at one time was the guard room for a now-empty admiralty service unit. I called to pick up a couple of fellows camping in a small forest of trees. Sometimes I was called upon to pick up lads that were sleeping in a coal shed at the local railway station.

The time spent eating and drinking beside the blazing fires at the hall, plus the club activities and personal help with problems, was always very deeply appreciated.

Buzz was desperate to find a job, but he was unsuccessful everywhere he tried. He eventually went to the car factory in Oxford who was willing to take him on, until they saw his hands. The factory boss said he could not employ him because he had severe dermatitis, which is inflammation of the skin with allergic reaction. Buzz begged for the job. The foreman in charge said grease would probably make the dermatitis worse but very kindly said that if, and that was a very big "if", the hands were better then he would reconsider the job application.

Buzz was very unhappy and sad as he told us the story at the club. "I have had this skin problem since I was born," he said. "It is not going to go after eighteen years, is it?"

Before I could reply another of the young men piped up: "Ken, you will have to pray about that."

One of the lovely things about the youth ministry was the way the young people saw constantly how God honoured faith and answered prayers. They had seen so many answers and expected a miracle every time we prayed. They expected prayer as the answer to everything, which was encouraging for me. I explained time after time that God has reasons sometimes to answer with "yes", sometimes with "no" and sometimes with "wait". I praise

God continually how He dealt with those youth problems and needs. Because of His faithfulness and mercy, and an abundance of His answered prayers, so many accepted Him for time and eternity.

I prayed every day for Buzz and the following week he returned with no change to his hands. His mates crowded round to look but the hands were no different. They urged me to pray on.

A fortnight later, on a different weeknight, I arrived at the chapel where I had taken on pastoral work in another village. I heard my name called as I fitted my key in the chapel door lock. I stood and watched Buzz climb off his motorbike from the other side of the road and walked towards me with his arms outstretched as though he was sleepwalking.

"Look at my hands!" he said.

I looked and saw the miracle. There were no red sores. I was looking at very white and lovely hands. God had done it again and a couple of weeks later Buzz got the job.

Sometimes I can see God's purpose in these types of miracles. Why was prayer offered to the Lord but seemingly unanswered and Buzz did not get the job? Then, why after more prayer, did the Lord answer with "yes" and he got the job? I saw that God had given Buzz the opportunity to witness the miracle he had received, to his family, the club members, my chapel folk and probably most of all his employer, who saw a miracle of healing for himself.

One could fill a volume of such wonderful things the Lord did for us at Garford. We can sum it up in a single text of Scripture, Psalm 119 verse 138: "The testimonies that Thou hast commanded are righteous and very faithful."

There is, however, a further miracle that God gave us

at Garford which I have retold to congregations around the world for decades. It really is a joy for it to be retold.

It was a normal night for Joyce and me to be doing the cooking for the Garford Mission Youth Club. The two of us were endlessly providing various drinks and frying eggs and bacon or producing beans on toast.

In the midst of all the activity one of the seventeen-year-old lads, Kim, came down the small flight of stairs to our small kitchen looking for food. I noticed that his hand and wrist were heavily bandaged and asked about the apparent injury.

Kim's story was very sad. During a drunken spell in Oxford he had seen his own reflection in a plate-glass window and, feeling sick at what he saw, he lashed out at the glass with a clenched fist. The force of the blow meant that he had cut a main tendon in the hand, which caused his little finger to droop, and the hand appeared to be paralysed.

Within seconds of Kim relating his story, the red glow of the electric ring on which I was making toast suddenly went black. It was obvious that there was no more heat and consequently no more toast or cooking.

Another of the lads, Ern, inspected the plug and decided that a couple of the wires were black and broken. "I can mend these," he said, and asked for a screwdriver which I could not provide.

By this time I was kneeling before a low cupboard to fetch out some more cups. As I knelt there I heard that inner voice which said, "Put the plug in the socket on the other side of the wall." Before I realised it I had repeated those words.

"It is no good putting it in another socket," snorted Ern

in disgust. "I shall have to cut off some wires and reassemble it."

I became very authoritative and said, "Put the plug in the socket on the other side of the kitchen wall."

Ern swore. "The wires are burnt out," he declared. "It is no good putting it in a different socket," and in disgust threw the electric lead on the table.

As I put the plug in the second socket immediately the electric ring began to glow. There was sheer amazement on the faces of the little group assembled and waiting for the food.

Em's face was a study. "How did that happen?" he asked.

I laughed and said, "I'm plugged into the chief electrician, Ern, and He performs miracles." They understood that I was talking about God.

Later that night, before I went to bed, I prayed and thanked God for the miracle with the electricity and the fact that He had allowed me to provide the food for them all. Instantly two words came to my mind: "Kim's hand!" I knew that God had shown me something more wonderful. If He could bring power through a dead plug and burnt-out wires, and to cause an electric ring to glow, by the same power, He could work through Kim's dead tendon to give life in his helpless hand.

Praying daily, until Kim came to the next club session, I asked him if I could pray over his hand. He was willing but scoffed when I asked him to put his fingers around my wrist and to squeeze it as hard as he could.

"You know I can't," he complained. "I've got no grip in that hand at all."

Nevertheless I repeated my request as he tentatively put

his limp hand on my wrist and tried to squeeze it as I prayed. He started to say, "I can't," again but within seconds his grip was so hard that it instantly bruised my wrist and I had to say, "Kim, stop! You are hurting me."

Kim relaxed his fingers and started to stretch and clench them again, looking at them very intently all the time.

It was a wonderful moment when he bounded up the steps, ran across the stage and jumped to the floor where the others were eating, drinking and activities were taking place.

"Look what I can do," Kim cried with tears on his cheeks. "Look what I can do." He repeated it again.

God had performed yet another miracle. In repeating it I can only urge everyone, who thus far have not believed or ever accepted Jesus, to put their weak hands of faith into the precious nailed hands of the Saviour. Through faith in Him we too can boldly say of Jesus, "Look at what I can do!", or rather, what He can do for us.

Sixteen

When so many of the young people got converted at the Garford Mission Youth Club, it became evident that we needed a church or some form of fellowship where we could gather on Sundays for a service. Where better than the village hall itself? We were the only folk who ever used the hall for youth activities. Consequently we prayerfully arranged an evangelical service for Sunday mornings and welcomed the villagers and some relatives and friends to join us.

The new services were well received and at the beginning of October we had a lovely harvest thanksgiving service. Villagers and friends from further afield supported us and contributed an abundance of fruit, flowers and vegetables which we had on display. We donated all the produce to a local Dr. Barnardo's Home afterwards. The following month we had a Remembrance Day service and laid some poppy wreaths at the village memorial.

We were given a lovely communion set and we were all set up for services except for one special thing that we needed. There was a lack of music for the worship and general hymn singing.

Once I had mentioned locally the need of an organ or

something similar; a friend told me of a chapel that had closed a few miles away in a village that I had never heard of. I was reliably informed that the now-redundant chapel was empty except for some old worm-eaten pews, an ancient Canadian harmonium and a piano that the last couple of worshippers were keen to dispose of. I was very interested in the piano for use at the new services at Garford. I sought out the couple who were sad to see their lovely chapel closed after it had been in existence for about a hundred years. Due to age and infirmity, and the fact the couple were the only worshippers left, they had no alternative but to approach the trustees who worshipped at a few other churches in the area for a decision to be made. They reluctantly agreed to close the chapel.

The elderly couple handed me the key to the chapel and directed me to where it was situated. They were unwell and unable to join me as I was invited to see the piano for myself.

The little chapel was well situated in the centre of the village. I arrived to find the front-door key would not turn in the rusty lock. I went round to the back door, and when I opened it, I found I was standing inside a very small kitchen.

I was sad to see the state of the chapel which was hideously painted half red at the bottom and half pink at the top. It had a wooden floor, which was so rotten in one of the corners that a couple of planks had been placed over it to take the weight of the harmonium. The windows were dirty and there were festoons of cobwebs and layers of dust. An ancient and broken coke stove stood in the centre of the building. The piano was quite a nice one and I knew I had come on a good mission. The Lord had provided a need yet again. I played the piano and then looked for the keys which

I had placed on it and promptly dropped them. As I picked them up I dropped them, and when I picked them up the second time they fell from my hands again. At the third time I headed to the front door which I hoped I could open from the inside because it had been impossible from the outside. It was at that moment I felt a tingling sensation in my body and an inner voice inside my head which said, "The keys of this place are in your hands!" I instantly dismissed the fact. I could not possibly take on any work in this chapel. I was secularly employed a long distance away. I was caring for a mother at home who was disabled with arthritis. I was already very involved with the mission youth club at Garford and now the Sunday mornings there as well. All this on top of an itinerant ministry in several places as I toured with the Lord in what I had called "His Ministry". I took the letters "HIS" to intimate "He Is Saviour" ministry.

I returned to the couple in the village to return the chapel keys and to arrange collection for the piano. Over a cup of tea this lovely Christian couple promised to tell the trustees that I wanted the piano. I thought I had made a grave mistake when I shared that I had felt the Lord was telling me that the "keys of this place are in your hands". They had conveyed that very thing to the trustees, and the secretary of the trust invited me to prayerfully consider leading or in some way helping out the cause in the village. I did not pray about it. I thought it was impossible for me to take on any further Christian work because I was already over-committed. I certainly could not see me in the role of a pastor of a church.

I did, however, arranged to meet the trustees at another venue for prayer and to thank them for the gift of the piano. Hitherto they had repeated their offer of allowing me the use of the chapel building if I could do some kind of Christian work in it.

Even for the sake of keeping another place of worship open.

I cycled to the trustees' meeting that evening. All the way there I was rehearsing my speech and reasons why it was completely impossible for me to get involved. My heart was beating when this little chapel's future came up on the agenda. It was time for me to tell them that I could not help. I coughed and cleared my throat, and to my utter amazement I heard me say one word: "Yes." I had no power whatsoever over my speech but to say that word.

I cycled home in tears. I told Mum of all that happened and she was as stunned as I was that I had taken on this commitment. Especially that she and I had discussed it so much for weeks. I had been adamant that I would not get involved.

I had said, "Yes," and now that I was committed, I had to wait on the Lord for the way forward. There were no funds available, no hymn board or numbers, communion set or even any hymn books, light bulbs or a dustbin.

The very next service I took in my itinerant ministry; a lady in the congregation was happy to hear that I had just taken on a new chapel. She felt led at that moment to give me a five-pound donation for it. It was enough money for me to obtain paint and paint the front wall of the chapel because it would be more pleasant to look at in pale cream colour than the gaudy red and pink. The problem was, when I painted the front wall, the remaining three walls looked even worse than before. At the next service I was given fifteen pounds and I reasoned that the Lord had again provided in His own wonderful way. Five pounds blessed the first wall face lift and fifteen pounds covered the other three. Money seemed to go much further in those days.

For several weeks I decorated the chapel, cut the grass, obtained necessities and advertised the re-opening chapel service on the last Saturday of June. It was so difficult to get any help. Every spare minute that I had, and my holidays from the secular job, saw the work for re-opening completed.

In my lifetime I have actually heard Jesus speak verbally four precious times. The first time I heard Him say simply, "Ken," when I had the vision of Him on the cross at my conversion. I retell the second time now, and the third and fourth times will be shared in a later chapter.

This last evening before the re-opening of the chapel I had just finished cutting the grass of the tiny lawn at the front of the chapel. It was the very last job before the re-opening the follow day.

As I wound the electric lead around the mower I sensed two things happening simultaneously. I saw the vision of Jesus walking beside me and entering inside the open front door of the chapel. He was dressed in white from the neck to His feet. I saw the back of His head, noticeably His long hair that seemed to glisten in the setting sun. As He entered the chapel there seemed to be a hush that could be felt even though we are situated beside a busy road with traffic. I could smell the sweet fragrance of honeysuckle and lilies of the valley that I have often smelt on other occasions when the Lord seems very close. Then Jesus spoke. He very quietly whispered, "Thank you."

I literally staggered inside the chapel porch and fell upon my knees in tears. There was no sign of Jesus. I felt the most amazing joy and peace whilst tears still ran down my cheeks. I felt so humbled. So unworthy. After all that the Lord has ever done for me, in sacrificing Himself on a cruel cross, saving me, undertaken in so many ways and never failing to bless and provide, how could He so graciously thank me for anything? It should be the boot on the other foot. I could never forsake thanking Him for everything He had done for me. Amen and Amen.

The little chapel was full and overflowing with people standing outside for the re-opening service on the Saturday evening. It was such a wonderful time and several people spoke of the Presence of the Lord in that place.

The following Sunday morning I had one middle-aged lady called Eileen at the service. We sang a duet and I prayed and brought the Lord's message just for her. It was the same every week for the next month, and the next, and the next after that. Eileen was the only solitary member of the congregation for thirteen months.

My Job's comforters started all over again. They started to say, "I was outside the Lord's will." "The Lord had allowed it to close." "Hitherto there had been no more support and that was the reason for closing." "God had no more concern for the village." "I was wasting my time."

I could have been so discouraged. I feel that so many Christians fall swiftly in defeat when they take their eyes off the Lord. When our faith and trust is tried it is so easy to be convinced that we have failed or that we have misunderstood God's plan. So many give in too easily and seem to fall at the first hurdle.

It is well worth remembering that we do not all reap on the same day that we sow. It is easy to serve the Lord when so much is provided and we can see the obvious way of going forward. I see that when all is going extremely well, or we are working to our own plans and agendas without reference to God, we are bound to fail and become despondent and discouraged. Remember, the devil is always active in his attempt to thwart the work of God and His followers. There is something wrong with the church if it is all plain sailing and without hurt or hindrances. The devil only bothers them that bothers him. The bigger the attack and onslaught of the enemy is overcome by the magnitude of grace and strength and the power of the Almighty.

We are encouraged in the Word of God, 2 Corinthians Chapter 12, where Jesus said, "My grace is sufficient for you, for my strength is made perfect in weakness!" The Apostle Paul replied, "Therefore I take pleasure in infirmities, in reproaches, in necessities, in persecutions, in distresses for Christ's sake: for when I am weak, I am strong." Jesus overcame every situation that He was called upon to endure.

We have His promise in Revelation Chapter 3 verse 12: "To him that over cometh will I grant to sit with me in my throne, even as I also overcame, and am set down with my Father in His throne."

It was a wonderful day when Eileen brought in two more friends she had met in the village. My congregation had risen by two hundred per cent in a single morning.

From small acorns oak trees grow, and from that day the congregation grew at a steady rate whilst the services at Garford village hall diminished. I felt led to cease the work there to provide opportunity to worship with us at the chapel. This was more feasible to stop preparing coal fires in two places at separate venues the same morning.

After forty-eight years the Lord continues to watch over His work in that chapel. He has done great things, for which we are glad. Precious souls have been saved, healed and delivered. Miracles have abounded. Couples have been married there within the beauty of holiness. Loved ones have died and been committed to the Lord in that place.

Amazingly, no-one could see the potential of that little chapel almost fifty years ago. Other parts of the Body of Christ did not realise the part that was hurting. Another part of Christ's body was being prepared for amputation and no-one cared except for Christ Himself.

I can never forget how the Lord Himself sent me on an errand to see a piano and through it gave the greatest privilege of serving Him for nigh on half a century and continuing. I wonder how many folk have similar opportunities, have been challenged but count the cost and missed out? I wonder how many are just content to "enjoy" their Christianity and not prepared to "endure".

Jesus is so gracious with His encouragement. St. Luke Chapter 12 verses 31 and 32. He says, "Seek you the Kingdom of God; and all these things shall be added unto you. Fear not, little flock; for it is your Father's good pleasure to give you the kingdom."

When water rates were introduced at places of worship we were given a large estimate at the chapel. We only had one tap in the kitchen. We had no toilet facilities but a bucket in an outside shed similar to our youth club at Garford.

I queried the bill. The Water Authority said the water rate was assessed against the rateable value of the chapel property. I challenged this because places of worship were not locally rated, but the authority kept ignoring all my queries and every six months sent me an ever-long and increasing bill.

It went on year after year with red demands and threatening of prosecution being levelled at me. Every time I prayed about it the Lord led me to some interesting topics. Psalm 25 verse 21: "Let integrity and uprightness preserve me; for I wait on thee." Psalm 40 verse 1: "I waited patiently for the Lord; and He inclined unto me, and heard my cry." I had to pray that God would make His judgement on His bill for righteousness' sake or provide the payment for it. I prayed as Jeremiah prayed in Chapter 12: "Righteous are You, O Lord, when I plead with You, yet let me talk with You of all Thy judgements." The answer came with added conformation: "Wait!" and, "When in doubt do nought." I realised I simply had to leave it in the hands of the Lord because the bill had rose to over a thousand pounds and we did not have anywhere near half of that amount. I was duly summoned to a court and to appear before a recorder to give reason why I had not paid the demands over the years. I was troubled with my conscience about going to law and appearing before unbelievers. I wrestled with the problems until I spoke long and meaningful to the Lord on my daily trips over the fields near where I live.

I had found a wonderful, isolated spot for walking daily with the Lord. In the heart of the country I walked over three fields until I came to the River Ock. A small and narrow river between rolling fields and where often cows gathered to drink from the water.

I had a set routine, with time kept apart every day for talking to the Lord as I walked through the fields to the river. Having spent some time where the cows drank, I then walked back to where I had parked my car. Then all the way back I kept silence to listen to His answers. Listening is so important. I was mindful of the twenty-third Psalm: "He maketh me to lie down in green pastures: He leadeth me beside the still waters." That was typically me. I knew on that excursion that I had to go to the court and I did.

I appeared before a very kind and efficient gentleman recorder and we waited for the representative of the Water Authority to appear. He did not. The recorder made several calls for the plaintiff, but there was no response and no appearance. It was just like the time Jesus was confronted with a woman taken in adultery. All her accusers disappeared when Jesus had spoken and He said to the woman, "Where are your accusers? Hath no man condemned you?" She replied, "No man, Lord."

Now in that courtroom there was no-one from the Water Authority to challenge or condemn me. No-one ever appeared. The recorder drew a line over the charge sheet and awarded the case in my favour. There was no bill to be paid and I was told that the court decision would be delivered to the authority. That action must have been taken because from that day forward there was never a word or a bill forthcoming from them. Is anything too hard for the Lord?

Walking back through the fields I thanked the Lord for His support and lifting the burden of the bill from my shoulders. In silence on the return journey I was reminded of His promise. Psalm 84 verse 11: "No good thing will He withhold from them that walk uprightly."

The Lord blessed me with a victory and so defeated the

devil. I could never have envisaged that day that very soon he would rise in revenge and attack with so much fury, deceit and evil. He was determined to cause the chapel to close for good and for me to stop ministering in it for ever.

Seventeen

To be the pastor of a village chapel is a grave responsibility. You readily acknowledge, and soon realise, that you are God's personal representative in that place. You step in as a shepherd figure, whose work is to care for and lead God's sheep to Jesus, Who is called "The good Shepherd: Who gave His life for the sheep". Shepherd and sheep being an allegory between Jesus and ourselves.

In St. John Chapter 10 Jesus speaks at length about the state of the sheep and the need to hear His voice. The pastor encourages the sheep to come to and stay near to Jesus because "they know not the voice of strangers".

Jesus continues to warn about wolves coming in amongst the sheep and scattering them. Typically this is the work of the devil, who constantly and endlessly comes to frustrate the shepherds and confuse and frighten the sheep. This enemy is never happier than when he is causing mischief, mayhem and confusion, in his attempts and endeavours to frustrate God's work and His followers. Peter, in his first epistle Chapter 5 verse 8, warns us, "Be sober, be vigilant; because your adversary the devil, as a roaring lion, walketh about, seeking whom he may devour."

It was a hard day, and a difficult time, when he led an

army and brought much ammunition with him to attack me. I was not prepared but betrayed and deceived and, perhaps most of all, saddened and disappointed that he tried to use my Christian brothers and sisters to assist him.

Our chapel was in a little circuit of four chapels when one of our sister chapels struggled to exist. All the trustees from the circuit of the chapels were preparing to resign at the time also. I was quite new to all the procedures relevant to the deeds of the buildings and change of trusteeships and administration and so on.

As far as I could ascertain one chapel was going to be sold from the group. In due course it was and raised more than one hundred and fifty thousand pounds. I thought, quite unwittingly, that we would receive a percentage of the funds received from the sale of the recently closed chapel. Prematurely I was thinking of redecorating inside and out of our building and to update the kitchen and install carpeting and to obtain a better organ. I thought the proceeds of the sale of the chapel would bless us tremendously and provide all of these things.

Law is a funny and unpredictable thing. I soon realised the meaning of Psalm 19 verse 13: "Keep back your servant also from presumptuous sins; let them not have dominion over me: then shall I be upright, and I shall be innocent from the great transgression."

A Charity Commission scheme conveyed our little chapel to a denominational trust a long way away in another part of this country. It also took several thousands of pounds, being a share of the assets rising from the sale of properties, with them.

The new denomination trust introduced so many

limitations upon us with the blessings of the Charity Commission. It was so legal and complicated, and none of us could make head or tail of it. It soon came apparent that we, at our little chapel, had now became the poor relations as far as the new trust was concerned.

I soon discovered, as well, that the new trust wanted us to undertake so many repairs and improvements to insure the building at its full value that it was impossible for us to comply. We had no funds and the trust had already received thousands of pounds from this district.

The new trust contacted a chartered surveyor to get reports and fire valuations for the chapel and billed us for several hundreds of pounds. On top of this our chapel was now responsible to implement all the repairs and alterations as detailed in the reports. Consequently with almost no funds the way forward looked grim.

After much deliberation and with very little sympathy, and what seemed to me no involvement with the Lord whatsoever, the trust gave me notice to quit the chapel. This chapel, just like our little sister chapel, was ordered to be closed.

I endeavoured to enrol prayer support and shared the news of our predicament with a lovely Christian businessman who got in contact with me.

This gentleman very kindly and generously offered the services of his own solicitors to help and advise us in our dilemma at his own personal expense. It eventually came to thousands of pounds which the Lord, through our amazing friend, blessed and encouraged us beyond anything that we could ever envisage.

The new trust continued to throw every spanner into the works. I was staggered at so much aggression and opposition that was levelled at us and me in particular. I was told to empty the contents of the chapel and return the keys. I refused because the Lord, in the first place, had said, "The keys of this place are in your hands," when He first led me there. Now, as far as I was concerned, He had never told me to relinquish the keys and that is what I told the trust. When they replied they also informed me that I could not fight their decision. It was pointed out to me that they were much higher than I because they were a large "Trust Limited" with the emphasis being on the "Limited". They appeared outraged when I responded and said that I had a larger "Unlimited" God!

The situation went on for months between the trust and our lovely Christian friend with his help through his own solicitor. The order to close and vacate the chapel date was extended month after month until I thought the most amazing miracle was presented to me. That day I thought God had answered my prayers in abundance. I had to acknowledge this was one of the greatest miracles that God had done in my life. It came days before the deadline of being evicted from our little chapel.

That particular Sunday an unknown couple came to our afternoon service. At the end of the service they brought me the breath-taking news that they had seen the notice advertising the sale of the chapel. This couple had called to assure me that they would purchase the chapel from the trust so that it could continue as a place of worship. The best news and evidence that God had honoured my prayers. I was overjoyed that God had undertaken in such a wonderful way. You can imagine my gratitude to God, and also to these His servants, who had called to bring me tidings of great joy. I embraced them both with joy and much thanksgiving.

Before returning home after the service, I rushed to the three fields by the river to thank God for His miracle and pray, and praise Him for sending His servants to purchase the chapel. I had not got as far as a hundred feet in the field before I heard the voice in my head and my heart. It was the Lord. He said, "This is not from me. Do not accept the gift!" I was rooted to the spot.

I did not know why. I could make no sense of this dramatic change of events. I was convinced, however, that I had to go straight home and telephone the friends to decline their offer. Sufficient to say it was not well received.

Within days the Lord revealed all that He wanted me to know. By another miracle I was introduced to a young man who attended the church in a secular building where my hitherto unbeknown benefactors also worshipped. He had sent me a spy. He revealed that the congregation there were unhappy at sharing the premises at a very secular place on a commercial basis. They were looking for a place of worship of their own and saw that our chapel was up for sale.

The Lord revealed their plan. These friends wanted to move in, take over and change almost everything we held dear. They were convinced that we would just move out. It was so hurtful that they believed, and said, we were not very spiritual.

We were accused of not speaking in tongues and that we did not embrace spiritual gifts of the Holy Spirit. It was generally supposed that God would most surely favour them in replacing us at the chapel.

Then God arranged an amazing turn of events. He led me to write to the Prince of Wales about our proposed eviction. My Job's Comforters started again, suggesting that would be a waste of time and I would only delay the inevitable.

His Royal Highness did in fact contact the hierarchy of the trust and everything changed dramatically from that day.

The Charity Commission, the trust, all our adversaries and critics, suddenly became over-zealous and supportive to ensure that we should continue worshipping at the chapel. No more demands for reports, no essential work to be carried out immediately and no more aggro. A complete reversal of all that had gone before, and not another word or sign of those who wanted to evict us.

They were silenced. Romans 8 verse 31 came very much to mind: "What shall we then say to these things? If God be for us, who can be against us?"

I learnt so many important things from these trials and temptations that God allowed me to go through at this crucial time.

First the devil is an old-time deceiver and he will use anyone, even Christians, the household of faith, to help him in his devious and evil ways if necessary.

As a young Christian I read in Psalm 118 verse 9: "It is better to trust in the Lord than to put confidence in princes," and I always thought that meant royalty. Then I understood that my Christian brothers and sisters are princes and princesses because the saved are heirs and joint heirs of the King of Kings. Born again of the Blood Royal. I was in fact putting my confidence in them. In my naïve way I never thought Believers could wander so far away from God and become tools of the enemy when it suits.

Jesus warns us in St. Luke Chapter 21 verse 8, "Take heed that you be not deceived." 1 Thessalonians Chapter 5 verse 21 says, "Prove all things, hold fast that which is good. Abstain from all appearances of evil." Whilst we are constantly reminded and warned of "false prophets, deceitful workers, transforming themselves into the apostles of Christ", according to 2 Corinthians Chapter 11 verse 13: "and no marvel, for Satan himself is transformed into an angel of light". How it behoves us all to continually seek the will and purpose of God. Not to be guided solely by Christian friends, no matter how well meaning they may be.

The many months of battle in our fight to keep our chapel from closing was waged against us from the Lord's people. That was more hurtful of all to me because I knew it was causing hurt to the Lord Himself.

It appeared that no-one was giving any thought that God had led His people to raise up that place of worship 150 years previously. No-one seemed to want to know that God was still working His purposes out. He was bringing souls to salvation and answering prayers. All they could see was bricks and mortar. An opportunity to sell and gain money. To be glad at having less responsibility for the Lord's house. No care for the souls or feelings of the worshippers. In short they were just as much in league with the enemies of Christ.

I know many were challenged when they finally saw the outcome of what the Lord had done in keeping His door open. Never for a moment did He stop saying, "The keys of this place are in your hands." I was, however, reminded of His Word in Isaiah Chapter 54 verse 17 and Zechariah Chapter 2 verse 8: "No weapon that is formed against you shall prosper; and every tongue that shall rise against you in judgement you shall condemn," because "he that toucheth you toucheth the apple of His eye".

Eighteen

I often say, "Expect great things from a Great God," when I speak about prayer and encourage folk to remember that He is able to do more than we can ever ask or think. I discovered that in a very special way when I made a simple prayer which God answered through a set of miracles. Moreover, He took me thousands of miles on a very special journey, gave me the joy of being on a special Service for Him and, finally, changed my greater understanding of His love and power, which changed my attitude forever.

It all started when I accepted an invitation to hear Richard Wurmbrand speak at a venue in Birmingham. Richard, his wife Sabine and son Mihai were living in Romania when the communists came to power in that country.

I heard first-hand from this pastor how he had been imprisoned for fourteen years. I listened to what he suffered for the cause of Christ. He was tortured and beaten and experienced appalling horrors all that time. Similarly Sabine was a slave labourer under the most brutal of horrors for three years.

In 1944 about one million Russian troops entered Romania and very soon after this the communists come to power in the country.

The Romanian Christians were totally deceived with promises that there would be no problems for Christianity and Communism to co-exist. Very soon, however, churches were infiltrated by secret police and the persecution of Christ's followers came in earnest. Churches were damaged, and meetings in private places were broken up with beatings and imprisonments. Individuals were tortured for their faith and dissuaded from attending Christian gatherings. Preaching and even owning Bibles and Testaments were forbidden. Brethren were encouraged to denounce brethren and many became servants of communism. Many disappeared altogether. I will never forget Richard Wurmbrand's closing words: "Friends, remember, evil comes in many forms. I see, here in Britain, you seem to toy with evil as though it is a fluffy baby tiger. Please remember, dear friends, that baby tigers grow up, and when they do, they eat you up." Solemn words indeed, which caused me to reflect on all that the pastor had said. He begged us to pray for the persecuted church behind the Iron Curtain, and I came home resolved to do that every day.

The words of Hebrews 13 verse 3 took on a very special meaning for me from day one: "Remember them that are in bonds, as bound with them: and them which suffer adversity, as being yourselves also in the body."

I prayed for the persecuted church, and especially for the Russians, that Pastor Richard and his family loved and witnessed to constantly in Romania. I prayed each day for just over two years. Then, at that time, the Lord never ceased challenging me about Russia. Every day it was something I read, saw on television, heard on the radio or people brought up Russia in conversation. It was constant.

Two very strange things happened in a single week. I heard from a Christian printers that they had printed a large quantity of Bibles and Testaments in Russian. I had never had any dealing with the firm and I had no idea how they obtained my address. I sent them a donation and said I did not want a receipt or acknowledgement but almost by return I received a large box of Russian Bibles, Testaments and tracts that I did not ask for.

Then into my letter box came an envelope of information from the area youth service concerning information and an application form, especially inviting youth club leaders to go on a cultural exchange visit to Russia. It stated they were looking for representatives from different counties in this country.

Now I was becoming anxious at the speed and the events that were coming in quick succession. Surely God was not asking me to go to Russia? Why was I holding so many Bibles, etcetera, then? I was reluctant now because I thought of the dangers, and there was still so much that had not been revealed. I decided I must have misunderstood what God was leading me into. I made excuses and a list of all the things that rendered it impossible for me to undertake this task. God very graciously led me in His Word to allay all my problems and fears.

One. What was the purpose for me going? I looked at all the Russian Bibles and Testaments and knew they had to go somewhere. John 15 verse 16: "You have not chosen me, but I have chosen you, and ordained you, that you should go and bring forth fruit: and that your fruit should remain: and whatsoever you shall ask of the Father in My Name, He may give it to you."

Two. How could I get into the country? I did not know anyone in it. There was that area youth office application form to apply for consideration for a youth cultural exchange visit to Russia. Surely they would be looking for folk to represent the counties? We were in Berkshire at the time because it was before the country boundary changes came in and we slipped into Oxfordshire. I imagined they would be looking for someone from Reading, Windsor or Newbury. After all, who knows where the Garford Mission Youth Club is in this country, least of all in Russia? I was a leader for a Christian club and undoubtedly that would not be welcome in a communist country.

I decided it would be foolish to apply. That very evening I was led to read the first chapter of 1 Corinthians verse 27: "But God hath chosen the foolish things of the world to confound the wise, and God hath chosen the weak things of the world to confound the things which are mighty." But I was still making excuses to God every time I prayed.

Three. But I cannot speak the Russian language. I continued to argue with God until I trembled in my bed as I was led to read how God dealt with Moses when he made the same excuse. Exodus Chapter 4: "Moses said unto the Lord, I am not eloquent… I am slow of speech, and of a slow tongue. And the Lord said unto him, Who hath made man's mouth? Or Who maketh the dumb, or deaf, or the seeing, or the blind, have not I the Lord? Now go, and I will be with your mouth, and teach you what you will say."

Four: I was secularly employed with the Ministry of Defence and I had signed the Official Secrets Act. They would never give me permission to stay almost a month in a communist country. Genesis 18 verse 14: "Is anything too hard for the Lord?" And 1 Corinthians 2 verse 5: "That your faith should not stand in the wisdom of man, but in the power of God."

I knew at this point that God had now made known His perfect will in that I should go to Russia. When I read in His Word, "Now therefore go," it would be disobedient to say no. I was very apprehensive, but I did say yes.

Everything fell into place like clockwork. I was accepted to represent Berkshire on the cultural exchange visit. The Ministry of Defence backed my application without the usual enquiries. Then when everything was going well, there was a huge diplomatic problem. Britain sacked several would-be spies in a Russian trade delegation here and sent them back to Russia. Russia responded by cancelling fifty per cent of visas for Britons to visit the Soviet Union, so there was still the chance that I would not be allowed to go after all. But God had other plans as I had my visa approved when fifty per cent did not.

We travelled by train to Dover, boat to Ostend and then by train for an overnight stay in Berlin. The blinds were drawn on the train so that we could not see out.

I peeped. I saw guards with dogs looking under the train, and then a conductor, accompanied by police, came into our compartment to check our passports. I was so thankful that they did not look in our suitcases.

The following day we entered into East Berlin and travelled to Schonefield Airport and boarded a Russian jet bound for Moscow.

I was the very first to leave the aircraft and walk towards the Soviet customs. I was joined on the walk by one of our group who had been with us for three days, but this was the very first time we had had a conversation. He was carrying a tape recorder and a lot of equipment, explaining that he was wanting to tape Russian music during the trip. The customs men pounced on him. He was adamant that there was nothing pre-recorded on the tapes he had with him, but the customs officers did not believe him.

It was my most nervous time as I stood before the customs. A group of them surrounded the man with the tapes, now checking to see what they contained. Nothing.

Because we were first off the plane, a long queue formed behind us whilst the customs played and checked several silent tapes. Other aircraft landed and passengers joined the ever-lengthy queue. Someone in charge started barking orders, and we were suddenly herded through the exit with a chalk mark scrawled on the outside of my unopened suitcase carrying the Bibles. Clearly God, Who can make blind eyes see, can cause good eyes to be blind when He has the need.

I went on several official cultural appointments at universities, art galleries and various other places. We travelled extensively to be present at endless receptions with my cargo of Bibles hid wherever I was staying. We moved on to various locations until God made His purpose clear.

Due to some misunderstanding with a batch of official appointments, I found myself with a complete day free from any engagements. I saw God had arranged this and I left the place where I was staying with a single Bible in my pocket.

By a very devious trick I "lost" my given Russian interpreter, Mike (so called because I could not pronounce his name in Russian), who insisted on never letting me out of sight or moving from my side. I devised a plan. I entered a shop and hastily left from the rear of it, and ran as fast as I could alone and as far away as it was possible.

I stopped when I could run no more and found myself standing beside a group of mostly women, at a bus stop. I mentioned in an earlier chapter in this book that I have heard Jesus speak verbally four times. First when he said, "Ken," when I was converted and the second time was, "Thank you," the evening before I went into the pastorship of the chapel. Now, here in Russia, I heard Jesus speaking for the last couple of times.

A bus stopped right at my feet where I was standing, and above the chatter of the ladies at the stop, I heard His voice: "I have set before you an open door, and no man can shut it." I smelt the unmistakeable honeysuckle and lily of the valley perfume and knew the Lord spoke from Revelation Chapter 3.

As though I was drawn by a breeze of cool air, like a magnet, I was drawn onto the bus. I put my kopecs (coins) into the little machine with no idea where I was going. I got off at another bus stop when I was the last passenger on the vehicle. As I stepped off, another bus arrived at my feet instantly and I went through the exact procedure as previously. This time the bus took me to the terminus, which was a very small country station.

As I was convincing myself that I must be going somewhere by train, the third bus arrived with the same drawing power, pulling me in. Passengers boarded and left the vehicle, mile after mile, until I was the last passenger and arrived at a place which looked like no man's land. The bus driver pointed and indicated that I should get off.

There was no sign of a living soul in this area. I saw a little lake, forests of trees on every side and nothing else but grassland. Why was I here?

Then I heard the Lord's literal voice for the last time. He said, "Follow you in my footsteps." I looked at a wooden gate guarding a sandy path which led up into the forest. I saw clearly the mass of footprints in the sand and followed them, seeing the onion-shaped dome of a church towering above the trees in the distance.

The church was surrounded by a wide clearing within the trees. I was amazed to find more than twenty people, mostly elderly folk, sitting on rough benches outside it. They stared at me and most of them smiled until two gentlemen came to me and asked me what language I spoke.

When I told them I was English one of them spoke to a third man who joined them. There appeared to be some argument as the third man kept shaking his head and looking at me very suspiciously. Eventually a tall thin lady, I imagine she was in her seventies, appeared with a warm smile and spoke in good English and asked me why I was there. "Do you visit churches in England?" she asked. I assured her that I was a Christian and instantly thought I had been very careless. It is not the thing you advertise alone in a group of foreigners behind the Iron Curtain.

It was now the turn of the lady to address the group of people. They started nodding and chattering and shaking my hand. At this point I withdrew the Russian Bible from my pocket. The result was electrifying as a very old man took it lovingly in his hand. I was suddenly surrounded by the entire group whilst the lady chattered very quickly. Two other men came up to me, one on either side, and I was frog-marched down a few stone steps to a small wooden door which seemed to open by its own accord.

I was led into a very small room and everyone, including

the men, crowded in and kissed me in turn. I looked puzzled until the lady explained 1 Corinthians 16 verse 20: "All the brethren greet you. Greet you one another with an holy kiss."

The lady was the only one who could speak English well. She said she would act as interpreter between me and the rest of the group. She also gave each one of us a paper covered in Russian and then put her fingers to her lips indicating that I should be quiet.

A younger man sat on a bench which was on a slant over the stone steps leaning down to the little basement. The door was shut and he sat outside it. Then the lady spoke in a very quiet voice whilst the rest remained very silent inside the room.

What a story she had to share. I was in the middle of a group of Christians which was a part of the underground church, meeting right under a crumbling building which was no longer a church but a museum of pictures and crafts and woodwork. I was introduced to the old man who had just taken the Bible from me. He turned out to be their leader. He fished out an identical Bible from within a pile of papers in the desk drawer and placed his Bible beside mine, and prayed over both of them.

There was some singing and prayers which was hardly above a whisper and then it was the turn of the lady to speak.

"You are Roger's friend?" she asked. "We thank God for him and for sending you to us with the Bibles he promised!" I shook my head.

It was then this interpreter lady gave her extraordinary story.

Six weeks earlier a young man called Roger had arrived at that same spot with two or three Bibles. He was not sure if he would be able to come again personally but he would try to send more Bibles with someone else. He could give no time limit except it would probably be within the next couple of months.

Those Russian believers had been meeting there by twos and threes, in faith and expecting to receive Roger's Bibles, continuously for six weeks. They were sure I must have been Roger's friend with the Bibles when I turned up. Without my mistaken identity I may never have discovered this underground church.

The problem that now confronted me was how to get the rest of the Bibles back to them?

The lady took me back to the bus stop where I had been dropped off earlier. We had to wait a couple of hours before the bus arrived and she took part of the journey to her home on it. She also drew a map and explained how I could get to and fro their assembly, and where I was staying, by taking two buses and a shorter route. Similar to Roger, however, I did not know if I could get back to them. I had cultural exchange engagements to fulfil and we were due to go on to another destination shortly. I also knew I would have some serious explaining to do to Mike concerning my long absence.

Sure enough, Mike, my bodyguard interpreter, wanted to know how I had got lost and where I had been. With a casual air and a warm smile, I told him I had been on a bus ride and visited a museum. I was reprimanded and then I was in for a further surprise.

Mike had been worried about my disappearance in case I was ill. Most of the group left behind had complained about stomach pains and headaches. It was decided that we were being overworked on too full a programme. More relaxation was called for. We would be split up in two groups for all further engagements. One group working whilst the rest relaxed back at home on one day, and vice versa the next.

Alleluia! That was just what I needed. On my relaxing day I would have the opportunity to deliver the Bibles where they were destined to be.

My return visit to the church was similar to the first. As previously the young man was sitting on the bench on the steps. As I approached, he stood up and pulled one end of the bench so that it bumped down the steps. That was his secret signal to a brother with his ear at the door inside the little room. The door was unlocked and I was admitted.

I discovered the sheets of paper were their hymn sheets. When unknown visitors visited, the hymn sheets were concealed in their clothing, to be hastily replaced by the minutes of meetings for the so-called museum. Services were sometimes interrupted by this procedure. Singing and hymns and prayers were whispered.

I saw tears of joy flowing down faces as the Bibles, Testaments and tracts were handled. I felt as though I would like to stay with them forever. The brief visit was far too short. I too was in tears that they were so happy in light of so much opposition and persecution. Would we in Britain camp out for six weeks in bad weather to receive a Bible? Would we be prepared to exchange an animal or some treasured thing for a New Testament? How brave would we be to endure what the members endure in the underground church?

There was a lot of kissing and good-byes as I prepared to leave. They had so many problems and anxieties, and all I had to worry about was facing Mike, my bodyguard, when I would have to explain another absence.

I often think of the lovely lady interpreter and all the love and appreciation of that little group of Believers as they gladly received God's Word. She wept as she waved me goodbye, but not before saying, "We pray for our brothers and sisters in the West. When you meet them, tell them we are praying for them constantly, and ask them to keep praying for us too." I felt so ashamed as I sat on the bus and they disappeared out of view. I had never heard anyone back at home praying for the persecuted church until I met Pastor Wurmbrand and Sabine in Birmingham, but they were continually praying for us. Too often we are concerned for very trivial things. We offend and get offended. We make mountains out of mole hills. Quite oblivious of the plight of so many of our Christian brothers and sisters.

I often wonder about Roger, whoever he may be. I guess he may have been sad because he was unable to get back with the Bibles he had hoped to take to that underground church. He may never know, until we get to heaven, that God did find a way. Who, or what, can ever stand in the way of the Almighty?

NINETEEN

In November 1992 the Queen attended a Dinner at the Guildhall, London, in honour of celebrating the fortieth year of Her Majesty's reign. After a year of ongoing disasters for her and the Royal Family, in her speech, the Queen said, "1992 is not a year on which I shall look back with undiluted pleasure".

Only days before the dinner there had been a devastating fire at Windsor Castle on 20th November. I had been given a God given prophecy to warn the Queen about His judgement, and the fire, at the beginning of August but, not surprisingly, no-one took the prophecy or the word of knowledge seriously.

I was heartbroken because there was so much unbelief and the warning was scoffed at. There cannot be any greater frustration than not to be believed, or for God to be dismissed, as though His views, warnings and judgements have no weight. How sad but how true; history often repeats itself in causing folk to say, "If only we had known in advance!" God is constantly warning us of certain judgements to come, but we do not heed them or even seem to care. We think we know best, even though God speaks clearly in Psalm 2: "Why do the heathen rage, and the people imagine a vain thing?

The kings of the earth set themselves, and the rulers take counsel together, against the Lord, and against His anointed, saying Let us break their bands asunder, and cast away their cords from us."

God, however, continues in the same Psalm to say, "He that sitteth in the heavens shall laugh: the Lord shall have them in derision. Then shall He speak to them in His wrath, and vex them in His sore displeasure." In other words, we can scoff and ridicule what God may say, but at the end of the day, He has the last word. He laughs and is in derision at our calamities. He knows how irresponsible and headstrong we become.

In spite of the foregoing, God is so gracious and merciful, that He warns us in advance and gives us the chance and opportunity to heed His Word and His Will. We often forget that He is omniscient in that He sees the future. We choose to ignore His word and then blame Him when things go wrong, even though Jesus made it very plain in St. Matthew 13 verse 58: "And He did not many mighty works there because of their unbelief." And so it was concerning the fortieth year of the Queen's reign and the fire at Windsor Castle.

Three times I had a dream that the Queen was weeping and that I was responsible. I had no idea why this was, but it seemed so real that I was urged to pray for her continually. In my dreams I saw that I was offering her the Bible, and each time I did this the Lord was saying I will tell you what to say to the Queen when you meet her with it. Without any hesitation, I just knew that God was going to bring us together for His very special purpose. He wanted the Queen to know the following, Psalm 95 verses 10 and 11: "Forty years long was I grieved with this generation, and said, It is a people that do err in their heart, and they have not known my ways: Unto whom I sware in my wrath that they should not enter into my rest."

The Lord gave me the first of the three interpretations. After a generation, in the fortieth year of Her Majesty's reign (1992), the nation was going more and more into sin and unrighteousness. Laws were being introduced contrary to God's will. The nation was embracing evil rather than good from the heart. Jeremiah 17 verse 9: "The heart is deceitful above all things, and desperately wicked, who can know it?" We were constantly turning our back on God. Our ways, our laws, invoked Almighty God's wrath, so that consciously we would not have rest or peace in our national life.

His Majesty King George the Sixth had previously introduced National Days of Prayer during the Second World War. God answered those prayers with miracles at the evacuation on the Normandy beaches, in the air with the Battle of Britain and finally in victory. All this was now seemingly forgotten and never considered necessary in the fortieth years of the Queen's reign. So God would give us a chance to repent and seek His face in prayer, so that we might prosper again.

Reminding us of Proverbs 14 verse 34: "Righteousness exalts a nation: but sin is a reproach to any people." Also 2 Chronicles 7 verse 14: "If my people, which are called by My Name, shall humble themselves, and pray, and seek my face, and turn from their wicked ways; then will I hear from heaven, and will forgive their land."

God spoke in the dream. If our nation still ignored God's Presence or His will in the affairs of the nation, He would bring justice to bear by speaking to our Sovereign Head of

State and declare His judgement on the nation by a refining fire.

The second prophecy was 1 Corinthians 3 verses 12 and 13: "Now if any man build upon this foundation, gold, silver, precious stones, wood, hay, stubble; every man's work shall be made manifest: for the day shall declare it, because it shall be revealed by fire: and the fire shall try every man's work of what sort it is."

The second interpretation was that God was challenging us about where our national foundation is built? Is it on a solid rock base since Christ is the "Rock of Ages"? Fire would reveal the good and the evil. Fire cannot harm gold, silver or precious stones. The alternative elements of wood, hay and stubble cannot last or exist when fire consumes it when judgement falls.

The third and final prophecy was where the fire of God's judgement would fall. He had already revealed that it would come to the house of God. 1 Peter 4 verse 17: "For the time is come that judgement must begin at the house of God, and if it first begin at us, what shall the end be of them that obey not the gospel of God."

The third interpretation was hardly necessary since God had made it abundantly clear. In the fortieth year of the Queen's reign the Almighty was grieved with this generation. He would test our values by the test of fire where it could only take place in the house of God.

Was it little wonder then that the fire fell, not in any one of the many rooms in Windsor Castle but in the Queen's private chapel in the fortieth year of her reign? Who could ever envisage a curtain in the chapel being ignited by a spotlight pressed up against it? Many will say a coincidence rather than consider it a God's incidence. I believe God moves in mysterious ways. A fire ripping the curtain in the chapel, so similar at the way the veil of the temple was rent from the top to the bottom when Jesus was crucified on the Cross.

Having received the commission to deliver the message from the King of Kings to Queen Elizabeth, I was faced with so many problems that only God could deal with. Who would believe the prophecies, the word of knowledge or truth that was revealed? Why are people so willing to doubt or believe a lie rather than the truth?

It was not feasible for me to pop in and see the Queen for a chat. With such a large volume of mail, she cannot possibly see but a very small percentage of it. What courtiers of the royal household, or ministers of the government, would be in the slightest interested or concerned? I tried to write it all down in my letter to Buckingham Palace.

In the first instance, when the Lord had assured me that I would be meeting the Queen, He instructed me to give her His Word. After prayer, I learnt that the wisdom given by God to Solomon was the same He was giving to the Queen, so I started to write out in longhand writing the Book of Proverbs. It was a much smaller volume of sixty-nine pages than the entire New Testament which was written years earlier.

When I completed the thirty-one chapters I had them all prepared for the binder to bind them in attractive blue hard covers with the words "The Queen" and "Proverbs" inscribed in gold. Then I felt God was urging me to collect pictures of all members of the Royal Family, which did not seem to make any sense to me at all.

However, I was amazed that so many people, at that very

time, were regularly giving me magazines to pass on to my housebound mother, who loved them. It was so noticeable that most of the magazines were full of royal pictures, but these stopped coming when I had collected several of them.

I planned to place the pictures inside the back of the book with the handwritten Proverbs on the top. Praying through every single procedure from beginning to end. The message came through very clear: "Your ways are not my ways, saith the Lord," as He led me to put the royal pictures on the top. God has a purpose in everything that He does.

I was in readiness for presenting the Book of Proverbs, with the warnings from God for the Queen, when I was faced with three searching questions. How, where and when?

Then in the weeks before the fire at Windsor Castle, I read in a local newspaper that the Queen was visiting Oxford on 3rd December. Her Majesty was coming to carry out engagements for the Bishop and Oxfordshire Diocese, open an Oxfam shop and tour the oncology unit at the Churchill Hospital. All within fifteen miles from my home and so convenient. I saw this as an opportunity and wrote again to Buckingham Palace because the Lord assured me, every time I prayed, that this was the day for our meeting and for Him to make His will known.

So receiving the Lord's assurance that I would be meeting the Queen sometime during her visit, I asked my boss at the Ministry of Defence to allow me a day's leave for the purpose. When I told him it was to meet the Queen he suggested I was a liar to my face. He asked me where I was going to meet her and I could not say. I had no confirmation (apart from the Lord Himself), no invitation or evidence, but the boss approved the leave anyway.

The night before the royal meeting, I reminded the boss that I would not be in the following day because of the Queen's visit to Oxford. He smiled and shook his head, and, turning to a colleague, said, "He has got no invitation to see the Queen. Who does he think he's kidding?"

It was six o'clock that same evening when I arrived back in the village where I live. I left our provided work coach at our village green. I started walking the short distance to my home in rain and complete darkness since we do not have streetlights in the village. I entered into my road of a row of twelve houses when, by the blinding light of a large limousine headlamps, I saw a chauffeured car with a gentleman sitting in the back. He was shining a torch light on the numbers of the houses. The car stopped when it came alongside me and the occupant wound down the window and asked me where my house was.

Within five minutes our meeting was over. The gentleman in the car was the Lord Lieutenant on a mission from the Queen. He had been instructed to contact me that day and to arrange for my presentation with the Book of Proverbs the following afternoon. I was advised about the protocol and the reason behind the gift. The presentation was to be the very last engagement at the Churchill Hospital before the Queen left by car for Oxford station and the train journey back to London.

It was a remarkable and wonderful day for many personal reasons.

I saw very clearly how the Lord had undertaken in every smallest way possible. Even the Queen coming so near to my home was a bonus. I saw why the Lord over-ruled my decision to put the royal pictures at the top of the book instead of at the bottom. Consequently the pictures of the Royal Family were the first to be seen. They took the Queen's interest immediately. As she looked at them, I almost felt like I was an old friend sharing the family photograph album with another friend.

The Word of God is especially precious to Her Majesty. I knew that afternoon God had blessed her and honoured His Word from Isaiah 55 verse 11: "So shall my Word be that goeth out of My mouth: it shall not return unto me void, but it shall accomplish that which I please, and it shall prosper in the thing whereto I send it."

On the way home I reflected on the way the Lord had undertaken in every single aspect of the presentation.

Before the presentation, the Lord Lieutenant apologised that I could not be included in the official programme of events for the Queen's visit because he did not know about it until the previous day, and I could not be slotted in at such short notice.

He apologised by saying, "I am so sorry that it must look like you have been added as an optional extra because you will be presented at the end." Not at all. It was the Lord's plan. If I had been presented during the day's events it would have been timed to the second. I saw how God had left me to be last so that the Queen's engagements were now completed. She was not preparing to undertake any other engagements and was completely free except for going home.

I was particularly encouraged with what the Queen did before she entered her car. Her Majesty declined the lady in waiting's offer to take the book of Proverbs from her, choosing instead to tuck it under her arm to look it again in the train.

The following day, 4th December 1992, I received two separate letters from the Queen's Private Secretary on the same day. The first said, "I am commanded by the Queen to thank you for the book of Proverbs which you so kindly presented to Her Majesty at Oxford. Her Majesty was most impressed to see this and congratulates you on it. She has asked me to send you her warm good wishes for the future."

How grateful was I for that first letter. It was my evidence and testimony to my boss that I had in fact met the Queen when he had been adamant that it would not happen.

The second letter from Buckingham Palace, fourteen days after the fire, thanked me for writing to the Queen. Apart from a personal greeting, the letter said, "Her Majesty has been very touched by the enormous number of messages she has received expressing sympathy and shared grief at the disaster that has struck such a loved and well-known part of the Nation's heritage. The Queen is only thankful there was no loss of life or serious injury and that most of the treasures in the Castle are safe, thanks to the quick thinking and courage of so many people."

When the Queen revisited Oxford in 2006 I produced a handwritten copy of the Book of Psalms for her eightieth birthday. This was not something I felt led to do as from the Lord but a personal gift. I just thought I would hand the Psalms to the equerry or lady in waiting, or even possibly a policeman in Her Majesty's entourage, in the hope that it would eventually reach her.

The Queen was opening the revamped Oxford Castle, now resplendent as a lovely hotel in the city. I just stood in the middle of a crowd of onlookers beside a dear Christian friend I have known for many years.

Again our God was very gracious. As the Queen was walking towards her waiting car, she stopped, looked in our direction and came straight towards us. Smiling and nodding at the bound Psalms I was holding, which were almost similar to the Proverbs I had presented to her fourteen years earlier, she said, "Is that something for me?" I again reminded her of our earlier meeting and she smiled and commented on the new pictures. My friend was delighted that the Queen then turned to speak to him and accepted a tape that he had brought along.

Another letter from the Lord Lieutenant, received a couple of days later, was very encouraging. He wrote, "I was very pleased to spot you in the crowd at the castle last Friday and see you presenting your book to the Queen. Your record of Her Majesty's response to your lovely work is delightful."

I never cease to be amazed at the way the Lord honours us if we honour Him. At the time of writing this book we have experienced many trials and tribulations. For well in excess of a whole year we have endured a worldwide pandemic of a coronavirus and other distressing tragedies and incidents on a global scale.

We are now just a few months away from the Queen's seventieth year of reign. If she is spared of God to continue to reign over us, may we ever thank and praise Him in uniting us in the national anthem of God Save the Queen. A time and opportunity of thanking God for His constant care and love over us. We are thankful to Him for all that is past and trust Him for all that is to come.

May our God also bless our Queen in that she may "Long to reign over us" and any hint of future speeches will no longer contain Her Majesty's words of 1992, a year of "annus horribilis". We eagerly look forward to her speeches to include "annus mirabilis", which is a remarkable or very good year for us and our nation. Thankfully, we can know this all the days of our life when we are part of the family of the King of Kings.

His throne remains for ever and His Kingdom shall never cease.

TWENTY

Many a day when I awake, I think of the words of Psalm 118 verse 24: "This is the day which the Lord hath made: we will rejoice and be glad in it." His mercies are new every morning. On this particular morning I was praising God for a very special letter that had arrived in the mail.

The letter was sent by a reader of my book *Road to Nowhere*. It came via the publisher because the sender did not know my address but was very keen to contact me.

The note, scribbled in pencil, simply read:

Dear Ken Stallard,
I read your book and I would like to meet you.
Please could you visit me next Sunday at 2pm?
Ron Kray

Although I did not know the man personally, I did know something of his history and reputation.

Ronnie Kray and his brother, Reggie, were incarcerated in two different establishments. Ronnie at Broadmoor in Berkshire and Ronnie in Her Majesty's Prison at Parkhurst in the Isle of Wight. Both were serving sentences for murder. Ronnie was receiving psychiatric treatment and Reggie was a Category A prisoner, which is very restricting, even in prison.

I re-arranged my programme for the next Sunday because I felt a sense of urgency in meeting Ronnie Kray. I was also very familiar about going to Broadmoor because of the times I had visited Pat from the Garford Mission Youth Club previously.

My first meeting went very well and the two hours for visiting seemed to fly.

Ron appeared in a beautiful pinstripe suit with a white shirt and silver tie. I noticed his expensive-looking shoes and beautiful watch and cufflinks. He looked like a very distinguished gentleman and greeted me with a broad smile with the words, "It is lovely to meet you, Sir." I agreed to call him Ron if he called me Ken. He smiled and insisted that I should sit at the table before he did.

Ron was very excited and full of praise about my book. He told me a story that came as a big surprise. He admitted that he had never read a book right through in his entire life. He had a little cunning plan going there in Broadmoor. He could liaise with friends, find tobacco and pass letters etcetera within the pages of certain books in the library. It was necessary to borrow a book to make his visits there look legitimate, but he never read them. Then he borrowed my book only because he liked the colour of the motorbike and rider on its cover. Ron said he started reading about the problem lads in my mission youth club and how they were dealt with. In short, Ron kept reading until he had read every page. I saw that God must have had a plan for him to choose the book and led him to read it right through. Ron was so taken with the truth of the story that he was most anxious to meet me personally. We spoke at length about God caring for the youth and how He had answered so many prayers. He asked endless questions about my faith, what the Bible had to say about a lot of issues, and how bad he was and how God would not do anything for him. We were getting along fine. I discovered Ronnie had a good sense of humour and was genuinely interested in my Christian ministry. I was deeply touched when he said how much he had been helped and he would read the book again. He took my address, promised to write to me and pleaded for me to visit him again. I received a letter every single day that following week and promised I would visit him again. There were so many questions he wanted answers for.

Days went into weeks, and weeks went into months. Ronnie's letters kept coming and my visits became more regular. We thoroughly enjoyed our meetings and the friendship and trust that developed. He drank non-alcoholic beer and smoked cigarettes, and I enjoyed tea and a bar of chocolate as we chatted.

A few weeks into our friendship, Ron told me a lot about his twin brother Reggie in Parkhurst Prison, whom he wrote to every day. A comment I had made to Ron had been very much on his mind and it was all passed on to his brother in his next letter. Ron had said a few times that God would not forgive him because of his violent and sinful past. My reply was that it was not up to me to judge his life, pointing out that Jesus said, "Judge not, that you be not judged," in St. Matthew Chapter 7 verse 1.

Jesus is the judge, but there is also mercy and forgiveness with Him if there is repentance. When Ronnie asked what repentance involved, I encouraged him to read for himself from my little Bible. St. Matthew 9 verses 12 and 13: "They that are whole need not a doctor, but they that are sick. I will have mercy, and not sacrifice: for I have not come to call the righteous, but sinners to repentance." When Ronnie asked again what repentance involved, I explained that it was not to be simply sorry for our sins. I had to confess mine to God in prayer, showing that I was truly sorry and, by a definite act of my will, to decide not to continue in those old sins again. I went on to explain that we all need to ask God to help us to live as He would want us to live, and we need to forsake the old ways. If we are tempted, have some besetting sin or habit, the best way is to starve it to death. Not feed it or look for it, but to actively turn away from it and seek God's help in prayer.

Ronnie was insistent that his sins were too bad because he had committed the worst commandment and commented on the sixth one: "Thou shalt not kill."

I tried to explain that there were no small sins or big sins with God. Sin was equal in God's sight. Anything that was contrary to God's Holy will in thought, word, action or desire is sin. The Bible tells us that the entire human race has committed sin and all of us have fallen short of the glory of God.

I showed Ron and encouraged him to read only four verses from Exodus Chapter 2 verses 11 to 14. Encouraging Ron to read the verses for himself, I explained the basics by following it up with a couple of short readings.

In short, Moses, being born a Hebrew, was brought up in the Egyptian Court as a son of the Pharaoh's daughter. When he became a man he saw an Egyptian beating one of his Hebrew brethren and retaliated violently. Moses killed the Egyptian and buried him in the sand. The second day Moses came across two Hebrews and asked them why they were fighting together. One of them challenged Moses by asking, "Who made you a prince and judge over us?" and then added, "Do you intend to kill me as you killed the Egyptian?" So Moses knew that his sin had found him out.

Ron never stopped listening but looked amazed when I explained that in the fulness of time, God not only forgave Moses's sin but called him to be a great follower of Him. Furthermore, he was chosen of God to bring more than a million of his Hebrew kinship out of slavery from Egypt. Then during the next forty years was responsible for leading them through the wilderness until God, by His miracle, opened the Red Sea for them to pass through. God finally led His chosen people until they finally arrived in their promised land of Canaan.

I concluded our little look in the Bible and said, "So, Ron, you can see that God receives a sinner who truly repents, as Moses did, and if Almighty God can do that for Moses, He can also do it for you too."

Ron's immediate response was twofold. First he urged me to promise him that I would get in touch with his brother Reggie with the same story urgently. Secondly Ron wanted me to give him the date when I could come again and show him more.

For a long time Ronnie and I met regularly and sometimes he wrote down questions awaiting my comments and answers. I felt the Presence of the Holy Spirit in our meetings, and I felt so happy sharing the Scriptures and taking all of his requests for prayer to the Lord. He wrote to me often with specific answers he had received and constantly begged me to visit Reggie. Sadly that was not so easy because I needed permission from the Home Secretary to visit a Category A prisoner.

Reggie and I were now communicating by letter several times each month, but that troubled Ronnie. He was anxious for me to meet Reggie in person.

The Home Secretary was Leon Brittan at the time and I knew that he was very much against the Kray twins. I decided that a letter requesting a visit for Reggie would probably get no further than the wastepaper bin. I needed a more personal, direct, face-to-face meeting. Then I believe God showed me an opening that could be possible. I decided to write to the Home Secretary about my handwritten copy of the New Testament and invite him to see it and add his autograph. I would take the opportunity of my visit to ask him personally to allow me to visit Reg.

Sadly the arranged meeting did not go well when I asked for permission to visit Reggie Kray in Parkhurst Prison. The Home Secretary declined my request, informing me that it would not happen "as long as I am Home Secretary". Sounding more brave than I felt at that moment, I took a deep breath and said, "Sir, I believe God has a purpose for me to visit Mr. Kray at Parkhurst. I am sorry that you do not agree, but man proposes and God disposes! I shall contact your successor." He never did sign the handwritten Testament. Instead he moved from the office of Home Secretary to be the Secretary for Trade and Industry, which was fatal for him. I was the speaker at a Full Gospel Business Men's Fellowship in the north of England at the time and I stayed overnight with friends. The next morning, after breakfast, my hosts handed me the daily newspaper. The headlines ran the story that Leon Brittan had the choice of being sacked or resign over the Westland helicopter affair. His removal was more swift than I had envisaged. I thought, "Who can stand in the way of the Almighty?"

When Douglas Hurd became Home Secretary it was time for rejoicing. Very soon Reggie was transferred from being a Category A to a Category B prisoner, and permission was given for me to visit him at Parkhurst from that day.

It was quite an emotional meeting the first time that I met Reggie. We sat at a table in a large community room where he drank pints of orange squash at a time. He appeared to be very slim and athletic, and I learnt that he enjoyed working out.

We knew so much about each other because of the dozens of letters that we had exchanged. Reggie was very keen to share me with how Ronnie was constantly talking to him about the Scripture topics. He was very pleased to receive a Bible, with a list of Scripture references available for almost every situation.

Although it was quite a long journey from Oxfordshire to the Isle of Wight, I enjoyed our frequent visits. Reggie was so generous and gave me a gift almost every time. Ronnie was similar with his generosity. When it was my mother's birthday they arranged for flowers to be sent. She was very touched by Reggie's gift of a handmade jewellery box. On one occasion Reggie gave me a most beautiful present which still has pride of place in my office to this day. It is a wooden, ornamental, cased clock with a trinket drawer, all made out of match sticks glued together and standing eighteen inches high.

The years with the Kray twins are full of so many

memories. Naturally I know so much about their past because volumes have been written about them. Some very violent, graphic and unsavoury. I have listened to their own personal accounts of events that took place. I have also seen evidence of the facts in some cases, which is quite contrary to lies and betrayals from some of their so-called friends who pretend to speak the truth. However, at the end of it all, I am not the judge. I can only speak from my personal experience of knowing and sharing with them.

It has been a tremendous journey. Their friendship has meant so much to me and God has taught me so much through them.

Did they become Christians? I recall the day in Broadmoor when Ronnie held my hand and said, "Ken, how do I come to be like you?" When I asked him what he meant, he said, "What do I have to do to be an evangelist?" I thought it strange at the time but told him what an evangelist is. I asked Ron, "Do you mean how to be an evangelist, or a Christian?" and he instantly replied, "A Christian." He followed me in a short prayer. Later in the week he sent me one of the tracts I gave him at a much earlier meeting and obviously he had kept it. It included words to the effect: "I repent of my sins, and trust you Lord Jesus to forgive me. Thank you for dying for me on the Cross, and today I invite you into my life to be my Saviour." On the dotted line underneath Ronnie had signed "Ron Kray".

When I told Reggie about Ron's signed tract, he asked me to pray with him, and I believe he was genuinely converted and dedicated. He wrote to me about people he was praying for and how much he was praying for Ron. He also said he had been praying for various friends both in and outside the prison, and he was seeing God doing miracles. Especially for the wife of a friend who had cancer.

We spent hours discussing the Lord, our hopes and aspirations. I also continued to witness the relationship that developed between Ronnie and a lady called Elaine in Broadmoor. He was very much looking forward to marrying her, and on the happy day, I was called upon to bless their marriage in a special room in there. In the process of time Ronnie and Elaine were divorced, and he re-married another lady, Kate, but sadly that ended in divorce too.

There was never a month went by without some momentous, or hilarious, episodes that I got involved with in connection with the Kray twins. Reggie mostly.

After driving to Southsea I went on the hovercraft to Ryde in the Isle of Wight. It only took a few minutes crossing the Solent and then I went on to Parkhurst Prison by taxi. Very often I was driven by the same local taxi driver. After a few visits, he thought he was jesting when he asked me if I was going to visit Reggie Kray because, in his view, Reggie was the most famous, or infamous, person in there.

During one of the visits, the taxi driver said he often read about the Krays donating various items and gifts for charitable purposes. He wondered, that because I was a friend, could I approach them to donate a special trophy for a winner of the local pigeon-racing competition? I promised I would do what I could.

Reggie was delighted to agree and said he would contact friends in one of his boxing clubs in London to make the necessary arrangements. The taxi driver was very pleased when I gave him the good news. I also promised him that I would collect the trophy from London when it was available.

Within the month I received a telephone call from the boxing club in London to say the trophy was now ready for collection. I was a bit concerned when the caller advised me to take someone with me because it would take two of us to carry it.

I had a very good secretary at the time, whose name was Adrian, and I was teaching him to drive. Adrian was happy to drive all the way there and back, where L drivers were allowed to drive except on the motorways. The sight of our faces amused the folk at the boxing club as we took the possession of the very large trophy and carried it together to my car.

Thick and very tall was a column, very similar to Nelson's in Trafalgar Square, that rose up from the centre of the large square marble base. A massive bird sat on top of the column which more resembled an eagle rather than a pigeon. Four similar birds, one on each corner of the marble base, completed the creation.

At the end of the week I had the task of conveying the very heavy trophy to Southsea. I struggled to lift it and placed it on the bonnet of my car. I collected other personal things together from the boot and, not thinking, I slammed the boot lid shut, and the vibration of the car caused the massive monument to crash to the floor. To my dismay I found the head of the pigeon, or maybe it was an eagle, laying some distance apart from the rest of the trophy. A quick call at the shops at Southsea, to collect a tube of Superglue, made the trophy look no more the worse for wear when I had finished my repair work on it. I had to enrol the assistance of a young sailor to help me carry it on to the hovercraft.

I duly delivered the trophy to the taxi driver at Ryde but

I never heard about it again from that day to this. I guess it's the thought that counts.

Reggie and Ronnie, in their many exchanges of letter, agreed they wanted to do me two very big favours. Ron wanted to contact friends on the outside of Broadmoor to raise funds for getting some good updated equipment for our mission youth club at Garford. Reggie, on the other hand, wanted to do something for me personally and to get his friends on the outside to arrange a party on a boat. It was called the *Princess Elizabeth* and it was moored on the Thames near Swan Pier close to the Tower of London.

Between them the Kray twins decided the party was to be in my honour because I had persuaded the Home Secretary to get Reggie off the Category A prisoner status. I didn't, but Reggie was always insistent that I had.

What a party that was. The friends of the twins worked very hard and there were celebrities present from the days of their former nightclubs. Charlie Kray, the twins' older brother, was there and he had previously invited me to do "something religious". After much prayerful thought I took along my handwritten copy of the New Testament and showed it to the guests. I let them peruse all the famous autographs in it. I closed my epilogue by saying that many people ask questions about the individuals who have signed it. Frequently they ask me of all the special encounters and experiences that I have had, who or what had impressed me most? I say, "Without doubt – King Jesus," and ended with a brief testimony. My little talk was very much appreciated and drew many questions.

One of the highlights of the party was when Charlie called for silence and ushered me, once more, into the centre of the room.

"I have been instructed by both Ron and Reg to invite Ken to become our adopted brother," he began. That was a bit of a bombshell and put me on the spot. "Ken has helped us so much and we now look upon him as a brother."

I just smiled and simply said, "Thank you very much. I am pleased to be a brother."

A murmur of approval and applause rippled around the boat. A few moments later, I could hear Charlie's partner asking, "Has anyone seen our Ken?" as she was looking for me. I smiled at the emphasis she made on the "our" and accepted that I was now, without any doubt, adopted into the family.

Our hosts on that boat not only gave us a wonderful party that night but presented me with a very generous donation of more than four hundred pounds. It was given me for the Garford Mission Youth Club, which was a lot of money in those days. All thanks to the Kray twins for arranging it all through their contacts outside.

The publicity surrounding the party on the boat, and how the proceeds from it had benefited the youth club, attracted the attention of Thames Television, who came to the village hall at Garford to film the club in action. The members thought that was amazing and felt like film stars when they saw themselves on television.

Since Reggie was now a Category B prisoner, he was moved around from Parkhurst to Gartree, Lewes, Nottingham, Leicester and Blundestone, and then Maidstone. Of all the establishments I preferred Maidstone best of all. The staff were extremely helpful and friendly towards me personally. Reggie certainly did not enjoy the same help and consideration there. Then sadly, however, after a year of Reggie being at Maidstone, his brother Ronnie died.

I lost a good friend in Ronnie when he eventually took sick and died of a heart attack. The Service was at St. Matthew's Church at Bethnal Green in London. There were very large crowds of people thronging the streets from Bethnal Green to the cemetery at Chingford. I was only able to spend a few moments to talk some words of comfort to Reggie at the funeral before he was escorted back to Maidstone Prison.

The weeks that followed were very sad and Reg's letters were full of reminisces of Ron. He was heartbroken at the loss of his beloved twin. Then, God moved in an amazing way and Reggie's life suddenly took on a very new meaning.

The first words he greeted me with on one of my visits was, "Ken, you've got to meet my very special friend Roberta." From that day on, most of Reggie's letter were full of details of Roberta's visits and how their friendship was blossoming.

Rob was just fantastic for Reg. They shared a wonderful sense of humour and their love for each other was very real and genuine. Reg loved Rob's stories from life and found her to be extremely intelligent and very good company. He lived every day in eager expectation of her next visit. I was delighted when in due course they invited me to officiate at their wedding.

Rob wore a beautiful white wedding dress and looked stunning. Reggie in his smart suit never stopped beaming throughout the service. We sang "Morning Has Broken" and "Amazing Grace" and after the vows I was able to pronounce them "man and wife".

Rob and Reg and all us guests had a lovely buffet reception at the back of the church in Maidstone Prison. There was an abundance of fruit and a beautiful wedding cake there as well. It was one of the happiest weddings I have ever witnessed.

Shortly after the wedding, Reg was advised of his transfer from Maidstone to Wayland Prison in Norfolk. I was sad to think that he would be much further away for me to visit, but I was happy with the thought that, after nearly three decades, he would be considered for becoming a Category C prisoner. Or better still paroled.

Letters from Reggie kept asking me to pray for the board that would be considering his parole. Reports were conflicting, dates changed and no-one appeared to be speaking the truth. It was a series of delays and frustrations. I felt so sorry for Rob and Reg because their hopes were dashed time after time. Rob was also present to love and support Reg at this very stressing time when he was so concerned about the failing health of his older brother Charlie. What a blessing that Rob was on hand when Charlie passed away.

None of us at this time could have envisaged that before the end of the year Reggie would be joining him.

Reggie's health deteriorated during the following months which gave great cause for concern. I sensed from his letters that he was struggling physically. He also wrote about his frustrations that so many of his so-called friends were either wearying him or, worse, were betraying him. Yet through it all, Reggie's faith in God, the assurance of his daily prayers and Rob, the greatest love of all his life, never failed.

He was surrounded by a lot of love and caring folk. This more than compensated for all the hangers-on, so-called friends who would not hesitate to cash in on him or seek the limelight.

Reg became more ill as the weeks went by, and Rob,

supported by some loyal friends, continued to stay strong to love and care for him, especially when the illness was confirmed as terminal. The only light at the very long end of a dark tunnel was that Rob was given the exciting news for Reg, that he had finally been considered for compassionate parole. It was public and it was true – Reggie was a free man! How I wished that Ron had been able to rejoice in that fact too.

Reggie's death was the end of an era. I had learnt so much from his philosophy of life. He was loyal, caring and compassionate. Over the years I have read, and been told, so much that is questionable, contradicting, glamourising and often a complete pack of lies. I can only speak personally of a man I found to be one of the very best friends I have ever had. I have a wealth of happy memories to last me a lifetime. It was an honour for me to give the address at his funeral. Apart from the passage of Scripture, I quoted from one of the verses of the hymn "To God be the glory"; it was simply: "The vilest offender who truly believes, That moment from Jesus a pardon receives."

During the years that I was a friend of the Kray twins, I lost some of my Christian friends. They considered them to be "undesirables". Some worried for my safety. Some questioned that I was helping folk that did not deserve it and consequently stopped giving to my ministry. Others scoffed, and on one occasion I got very angry when a man muttered to his friend, "Birds of feather, flock together," and questioned my motives.

In conclusion, what else can I say apart from what Jesus Himself said on many of life's issues, including, "I was sick, and you visited me, I was in prison, and you came unto me. Then shall the righteous answer Him, Lord, when saw we you sick, or in prison, and came unto you?" Jesus said, "Inasmuch as you have done it unto one of the least of these my brethren, you have done it unto me." St. Matthew Chapter 25. There, then, lies the answer for my motive.

TWENTY-ONE

I have always been very challenged by what the Apostle Paul said in 1 Corinthians 9 verse 22: "I am made all things to all men, that I might by all means, save some." I believe every Christian has a God-given gift and endless opportunities to speak up for Him and to be a living witness. Whenever opportunities arise to "gossip the gospel" or give a personal testimony of something good that God has done for me, or answered some specific prayer, I like to have something scriptural to hand out to others. For this purpose I like to carry a good gospel tract, or a little Christian booklet, to pass on with details of where any further information can be obtained and where help is available.

More than thirty years ago I felt led to write a very special tract for hitch-hikers. I always looked forward to long journeys on my itinerant ministry and, in those days, it was a familiar sight to see folk thumbing for lifts at roundabouts and on junctions to motorways. I loved the company of strangers on the journeys. It was always a good opportunity to turn the conversation to spiritual things. I never failed to offer a lift to anyone who was thumbing. Indeed, I used to pray for God to put hitch-hikers my way.

Very sadly there are so few hitch-hikers nowadays.

Drivers are anxious about offering lifts, and folk that are hiking are nervous to get into vehicles with strangers. There seems to be so much fear and uncertainty about what could happen on the journey. It is not safe because there are so many individuals who prey on vulnerable folk for sexual motives, or to rob, threaten, terrify or even force you out of your own car. Drivers have been forced to get out of cars, abandon you and the hitch-hiker drives away. For these and other reasons I no longer have a ministry to hitch-hikers for my own safety. Similarly, it is not a familiar sight to see anyone thumbing a lift now. There is too much distrust on either side.

I must have handed out about a thousand of my personal tracts, "Hitch Hiking to Heaven?", during the days when I felt completely safe to do so. I also recall the hundreds of times I have been the hitch-hiker, especially when in my RAF uniform, and when I was thumbing for lifts between home and the units where I was stationed.

When I was giving lifts to folk that wanted it, I got into some amazing conversations.

I can only recall a couple of incidents when travellers refused the tract when they arrived at the point where they wanted to be dropped off. The others stuffed them into their pockets or bags and only the Lord can know the rest.

In the tract I wrote that hitch-hikers are liable to miss their way. They would not want to be taken in the wrong direction. There are many ways open for the journey, but only one way to Heaven and that is through Jesus.

Loaded down with travelling gear hampers our progress, so it is a relief when the burden is transferred to a car. How similar to Jesus taking our burden of sin. Finally, we cannot thumb our way to Heaven, but Jesus can ensure we get there if we are on the right way today. Jesus said, "I am the way, the truth and the life, no man cometh to the Father but by me." At the end of the tract I wrote, "If you have been helped by this leaflet or require further help, please contact me." I provided my contact address.

Over the years I received many letters thanking me for providing lifts and sharing my testimony. I heard how some of the folk got further lifts, and all kinds of help, after they left me and continued hitch-hiking on to their destination. It was nearly always the same story. They had received some unexpected lift, or some particular help, which they attributed to the fact that I had promised to pray for their onward journey.

There were dozens of exciting encounters. I once picked up a well-known jockey who had been in an accident and his car was written off. I went on a little detour to take him home, where he insisted I went in to see all the cups, trophies and medals he had won through his profession. He also opened up about having very sad personal circumstances. He asked me to pray with him until the early hours of the next morning. I was able to leave him with a gospel card with the words: "Take my yoke upon you, and learn of Me, for I am meek and lowly in heart: and you shall find rest unto your souls. For my yoke is easy, and My burden is light." St. Matthew 11.

I was heading away from my chapel late one evening when I met an old gentleman staggering towards me in a heavy snowstorm. He was wearing an old ragged overcoat, a balaclava hat and carrying two heavy-looking carrier bags of possessions. We were a long way from any form of shelter. I turned my minibus around and stopped to pick him up because he was going in the opposite direction. I had to lift the man up into my minibus because he could not lift his feet up as far as the high step into the vehicle. He wanted to know if there were any barns he might be able to sit in until daylight when, hopefully, the snow would stop falling.

I discovered his name was Joe; he was homeless and was heading for the lights of Oxford.

I took him back to my own chapel, late in the evening, and sat him down in the schoolroom. I had been there earlier in the evening and it was still warm from the central heating. I made him a cup of tea and gave him some biscuits. As I was making the tea he shuffled to the bookstall and picked up a Bible. I said he could have it and he was delighted as he popped it into one of his paper bags.

"Do you think you can do anything for my feet?" he asked. It was then I saw the old worn boots and very ragged socks which were oozing with blood. I saw he had ulcerated legs and raw feet, with more blood, seeping with wet matter, and I was sure there was gangrene there because of the foul smell.

It took some time to produce hot water and clean up his feet and shins. A torn-up towel was used as bandages, kept in place by elastic bands in lieu of safety pins.

He didn't argue but seemed very pleased when I insisted I was taking him to hospital. Poor old Joe. He thanked me over and over for the gift of the Bible and promised that he would look after it and read it as I left him with a nurse and a young doctor.

I called at the hospital the next day to see how Joe was doing, but he had discharged himself and I never saw him again. I trust that his feet may now be "shod with the preparatian of the gospel of peace" according to Ephesians 6 verse 15, and that his new Bible might indeed be his compass and guide to lead him to a place reserved in Heaven.

During the years that I picked up hitch-hikers, I often found that they started the conversations on spiritual matters. They saw the little cross on the dashboard, or picked up a tract in the car pocket, which led on to good discussions.

Neil was such a hitch-hiker who read the tract and asked questions. It was another of those God appointments because all that week different folk had been talking to him about the Lord. We travelled several miles until we came to the point where he wanted to go on in a different direction. He seemed reluctant to leave the car and said he was returning to a university. I was delighted when he promised to search out a Christian at the university and took several tracts.

A few miles on and it was time for Neil to leave the car and to take on another route. Neil was out of the door now and was standing outside it. He thrust his hand deep into the pocket of his jeans and withdrew some coins and hastily counted them. "Will you please accept this?" he asked. "I'm afraid it is only fifty-eight pence, but it's all that I've got, and it is worth it for all that you have told me tonight. Please put it in the next church collection." I insisted he kept the money and I believed that the Lord would undoubtedly add to it. I was deeply moved by the sincerity of his offer. I drove away thinking of the widow's mite in Scripture. I recognised that in Neil's estimation, the knowledge of salvation was worth all that he had.

Sometimes the Lord led me to pick up vagrants in order that He could teach me valuable lessons from them. Barry was such an instrument in the Master's hands. The homeless lad, in his twenties, was hitch-hiking around Oxfordshire endeavouring to do little jobs to earn some money where he could.

I gave him a lift to a village some distance from where I live on a Saturday evening. He was hungry and had no money. I got us both some food from the local fish and chip shop and headed for his lodging. On the way he explained that he was living in a storage shed in the middle of a large fruit orchard. The owner had allowed this casual fruit picker to stay in the shed and sleep in the hay within it.

Barry had expected to receive his wages for the fruit picking on the Saturday I gave him the lift. However, he was disappointed because he had found the wages were not paid until Mondays for casual labourers. This practice ensured that there was a labour force on Monday mornings, and that the fruit pickers did not disappear at the weekends.

I promised to pick up Barry the following day and bring him home for Sunday lunch and tea with my mother and myself. This pattern followed for at least a month. I took him to chapel every Sunday and to the mission youth club during the week.

Barry did repairs on my minibus and helped at the club and did everything possible to repay our hospitality. It continued until the day of our harvest thanksgiving service.

Unbeknown to me, Barry had gone to his employer and asked him if he could have some of the pears and plums he was picking for our harvest thanksgiving service. He wanted it to be his offering. He was given permission to pick up some of the fruit that had fallen off the trees. The fruit was not for picking. This upset the lad and he complained. "It seems terrible to me," he said, "that God Who provided the fruit in the first place cannot have it straight from the tree."

As I was getting ready for the thanksgiving service that evening, Barry was at the sink carefully washing and delicately drying every individual pear and plum, then carefully placing them on display in a new box. It took ages and I became impatient, thinking he would get me late for the service.

"Come on, Barry," I urged. "You have not got time to wash it all, put it in the box as it is."

His face was a study. He looked me in the eye and quietly replied, "The Lord deserves the best," and he continued to wash and prepare every plum and pear.

I accepted the chastisement. The Lord certainly deserves the best we can offer. The Lord, that very thanksgiving day, led me to read Hebrews 13 verse 15: "By Him therefore let us offer the sacrifice of praise to God continually, that is, the fruit of our lips giving thanks to His Name." Barry not only gave the Lord his fruit that night, but in the process of time, he gave Him his heart also.

If you are undertaking a specific journey regularly, and at the same particular time, you sometimes come across an individual thumbing for a lift. I did not think it was unusual when I picked up a young man at a roundabout.

He grinned as he picked up my Bible from the passenger seat and placed it on his lap, and asked, "Are you a Bible basher?"

"No," I replied with a smile. "It's a fairly new one and I don't want to bash it just yet." The lad thought it was funny and I smiled at his next question.

"Do you believe in God and all that?" he enquired, and before I could answer he went on, "Do you think He answer prayers?" When I confirmed both questions with a, "Yes," he got quite serious and muttered, "Could He answer a prayer for me then, because I have got a problem?"

I assured him that God answers all prayers. Sometimes with, "Yes," sometimes with, "No," and oftentimes with, "Wait," but He is always on speaking terms with us when we speak to Him. He knows what is best for us.

I asked him what his name was and made a mental note of Duncan. I then asked him what his problem was. I was aghast when he said, "It's none of your business. I am not telling you." Then Duncan continued, "If He is God, surely He will know what my problem is."

Again, another challenge from the Master. From that day I have always made it a very strict rule not to ask personal questions. I could cause embarrassment. I do not want to pry, but above all, I don't want to put my thoughts to God but seek His face and His counsel. It is not up to me to guess, or ask, what the problem might be. It is up to God to reveal it.

I felt rather humiliated at Duncan's attitude, but I promised I would ask God simply to help him overcome the problem he was having difficulty with.

"Will you be coming this way again next Tuesday at about the same time?" Duncan asked. "I am on a day release study course in Oxford every Tuesday. I am in walking distance from the classroom and I could meet you here if you agree."

"Yes," I agreed. "I am on my home from my secular job every day at the same time. If you are waiting, I will give you a lift as far as the place where you need to change the route."

Duncan got out of the car with a startling remark. "I can't wait to see if your prayer works this week," he said. "See you next Tuesday. Same time," and with a wave he was gone.

For the rest of my journey, and later that night, and sometime each day, I prayed for Duncan and whatever his problem might be. I knew that Duncan would be convinced for Jesus's sake if he understood how He was dealing with his situation. I needed the Lord to reveal the answer that I was seeking.

There is no question that we have where there is no answer in the Bible. I thought of how Daniel reasoned with King Nebuchadnezzar: "There is a God in Heaven that reveals secrets," according to Daniel Chapter 2 verse 28. Daniel was accustomed of going into his house, kneeling by his windows, which were opened towards Jesusalem, and praying three times a day. God rewarded his prayers and revealed secrets as a result. I reasoned that if God can do it for Daniel, He can also do it for me, as I took on board Daniel's attitude.

Before the end of the week I heard myself praying: "Dear Father, I ask in Jesus's Name, will you please bless Duncan and heal him from wetting the bed?" Amazing! I had the answer about what the problem was before I asked. This took on a complete new meaning of Isaiah 65 verse 24 for me: "And it shall come to pass, that before they call, I will answer: and while they are yet speaking (praying) I will answer."

Praise God, He had revealed Duncan's problem. All I had to do was to pray about it. I felt excited and looked forward to my next meeting with the young man.

Sure enough, Duncan was waiting for his lift at our pre-arranged spot. He greeted me with, "You've been praying for me," as he climbed into the car. Grinning from ear to ear, I asked him if his problem was better. He said, "Almost one hundred per cent," with the adage "It's a miracle!"

I made what I thought was a mistake when I said, "Well,

your problem was not a problem for God. It was not so great a problem anyway, was it?"

Duncan disagreed and said, "It was a gigantic problem for me."

In the conversation that followed Duncan declared, "Well, you don't know what the problem was," and, in retrospect, I felt it was unwise because I said, "I think I do."

He insisted on asking me to name the problem and I did. Again, I didn't anticipate Duncan's reaction. It was similar how, as it had been in the first place, he refused to reveal it by saying God must know and it was not for my hearing.

Now the young man was clearly embarrassed and demanded to know who had told me about his problem. It was difficult to explain how the revelation had come to me. It is so difficult to explain spiritual things to the unspiritual. However, I did assure him that it was nothing to do with me but God looking out for him. Duncan's started smiling again when I said, "I am only the postman, thank the One Who answered your prayer."

As I dropped Duncan off at the dropping point he said, "See you next week," and then very quietly added, "Keep praying for me."

I did pick up Duncan every week for the next couple of months. He first confirmed his problem was resolved almost a hundred per cent. I kept praying as promised. By the end of his course and hitch-hiking days were over, he was rejoicing that the problem had disappeared altogether. For the first time in all of his seventeen years. He was so thankful and appreciative of our journeys during his course. What a great and glorious God we have!

I never saw Duncan again, but it had such a lovely

postcript. His mother found my tract, bearing my address, in his room. She knew all the details about our conversations and wrote to send her thanks, with his, for all the lifts and for the prayers. She concluded with the words: "It has made such a big difference to his life and ours."

We should never under estimate the value of a tract. Especially the ones that are anointed of the Holy Spirit. It is like seed that is sown on good ground. Jesus said, "It is he that heareth the word, and understands it; which also beareth fruit, some an hundredfold, some sixty, and some thirty."

God grant that we may continue to sow the seed of His Word in this needy world. Ecclesiastes 11 verse 6 encourages us: "In the morning sow your seed, and in the evening withhold not your hand: for you know not whether shall prosper, either this or that, or whether they both shall be alike good." It is as Ecclesiastes 11 verse 1 promises: "Cast your bread upon the waters: and you shall find it after many days."

Twenty-two

I am so glad that we do have the Christ for every crisis because there have been so many crises in my own life. In retrospect, I have seen the Lord's hand of protection or undertaking on every occasion.

I was only twenty-four when I had a serious accident whilst riding as the pillion rider on a very good friend's motorbike. His name was Mick and he offered to give me a lift as far as my grandmother's home. It was his intention to travel further on to meet his girlfriend after he had dropped me off.

Mick arrived later than we arranged. This was well before the time of mobile phones, at a time when so many did not have telephones in their homes, and one relied on contacting folk from one telephone kiosk to another.

On this occasion, Mick said he would phone the girl at her kiosk at the time previously arranged. He would confirm that he was on his way to meet her, but his arrival would be later than anticipated. To be able to do this, he proposed to telephone from a kiosk en route to my grandmother's home.

We had only travelled about four miles on very poor country roads before we encountered a problem. A farmer was herding along dozens of cows which took up the entire width of the road. They were being taken from a field to the farm for milking.

It was a long distance from field to farm. It was impossible to get past the cows and consequently we had to creep along behind them, which seemed to take ages. Mick began to get agitated. He thought that his girlfriend would stop waiting so long for his call, and he would miss the opportunity to say he had been delayed. Once the cows were herded into the farmyard, Mick opened up the throttle on the motorbike and we were travelling at a speed which I thought was far too fast. It really was a case of more haste but less speed.

I remembered hearing a very loud bang. I also recalled Mick screaming as I was catapulted through the air and landed on my face at the verge of a grassy bank.

I was conscious of the motorbike laying on its side several yards distance away, as Mick hobbled, with a damaged knee and bleeding hands, to where I was lying.

I saw the green grass turning red as the blood from my face dropped on to it. I remember I was crying, "I'm not dead. I am not dead," as I was trying to convince myself of the fact.

A motorist came along and promised he would call at the farm to telephone for an ambulance. He was heading in the same area where Mick lived. When the ambulance arrived he took Mick home whilst I was taken to hospital in Oxford. I arrived home very late that evening with my face and head swathed in bandages. When there was a good degree of healing, I was re-admitted to the hospital's department of plastic surgery. I received surgery to clean out some crushed bone in my eye socket, repair to my lip and to remove a scar from my cheek. Tar from the road had got into the scar and so it looked as though my face had been tattooed.

Although my face was a mess the Lord gave me an amazing healing. Nowadays the scar can only be discerned when my face gets cold.

Mick emigrated to Australia a little while after the accident and we have not seen each other for many years. He never ceased apologising to me for my injuries as he felt so responsible for the accident. The police said he did not have sufficient air in the tyre so that it exploded.

I think about the accident whenever I pass the spot. It reminds me of Proverbs 27 verse 6: "Faithful are the wounds of a friend; but the kisses of an enemy are deceitful." Tragedy can be a wonderful tool for deepening friendships.

I never cease to be amazed how so many blessings can come out of a single tragedy. It is a fact that when Christ is in the boat, we can laugh at the storm.

It was a very dark night in December when I left home to drive a very long way to Brecon in Wales. I had been booked to be the speaker at a businessmen's Christmas dinner, but I had only driven six miles from home before the accident happened.

Without any warning my car lurched sideward. The car hit the verge, caused me to somersault twice and skid at an alarming rate upside down on wet grass. With a sickening thud I ended upside down in a ditch with the side of the door against a tree. During the event I got tangled in the seat belt so that it seemed as though I was being strangled. Hanging upside down, I could do nothing to help myself and petrol was pouring out from the engine. This was the very point that God chose to perform several miracles in quick succession.

A couple of young men following behind me had witnessed the accident. They came to my rescue and released me from the seat belt. Because of the position of the car in the ditch, the lads brought me out through the boot.

A police car was the next vehicle on the scene and stopped to see what had happened. The officer shone his torch on the skid mark in the grass and saw the condition of the car as I explained that I was now free and fine. To which he said, "Someone up there must love you," to which I wholeheartedly agreed.

The policeman pointed out that the skid mark looked as though the car was heading straight for the tree. It was as though a hand had pushed it aside so that it ended up at the side of it. The man spread apart his thumb and fingers so that his thumb was on the car and his little finger on the tree. "You missed certain death there by six inches," he explained. "If you had hit the tree head-on you would have broken your neck, or strangled yourself by the seat belt. It's a miracle!"

The two Samaritans who came to my rescue very kindly offered to drive me home. I needed to phone the friends at Brecon to cancel my appointment with them.

Miracle number two, was that the two men who rescued me had an astonishing story to tell as they drove me home.

They were two young Christians who had been present at a fellowship meeting that week, and they had been listening to a gospel cassette tape I had recorded. Both agreed that it was incredible that they had heard me speak so recently and pick me up as they did. We formed a bond that very night and we had fellowship several times afterwards.

Whilst I was without the car, one of the young men drove me to speak at a meeting on the coast and actually gave his own testimony at the meeting. The same young man was a serving airman and a photographer in the Royal Air Force, and produced some lovely professional photographs for the ministry.

Miracle number three came in the form of the local newspaper report about the accident. It was under the heading "Miracle escape for Evangelist". I liked that because it gave God the glory for it.

The fourth miracle came via a telephone call. The caller said he was acquainted with my ministry and had read the newspaper report about the accident. He went on to say, "Now you have lost your car, how will you be able to get out on the Lord's work?"

I reminded this person of Philippians Chapter 4 verse 19: "But my God shall supply all your need according to his riches in glory by Christ Jesus," and I felt that if God still wanted me to work with Him, He would find a way. The caller agreed.

He asked me if I knew about a car showroom not far from where I live and, if so, could I be there at 11am on Saturday? I agreed to both. When I asked the caller who he was, and how did he know me, he rang off.

Miracle number five became apparent when I duly arrived at the showroom as instructed and found a brand-new car waiting for me.

It had been left by a customer who insisted on being anonymous. The salesman had been bound by secrecy as part of the deal. So, I drove off in a brand-new car. I had no idea who had arranged it, but I certainly knew Who had provided it. Proving yet again Psalm 84 verse 11: "No good thing will He withhold from them that walk uprightly."

God's protection, used to increase my faith in Him, has been very evident in my life's experience as well. Never more so as it is revealed in 1 Peter 1 verse 7: "That the trial of your faith, being much more precious than of gold that perisheth, though it be tried with fire, might be found unto praise and honour and glory at the appearing of Jesus Christ."

My faith was very tried and challenged when I came home from work on a bitter cold March afternoon and found my home ablaze.

I had taken retirement from the Ministry of Defence to take up working in a nursing home which is quite near to my home, and even closer to the chapel where I am the pastor.

This was a twofold exercise. First, it was only a fraction of the former daily journeys to and fro the government job, and it was only part time. I needed fewer working hours because of my extended Christian ministry. I also enjoyed my new job as the home activities co-ordinator, working with mostly elderly people unable to look after themselves.

I enjoyed arranging for indoor and outdoor activities, games and outings and various entertainments. I played the piano for the residents and we used to sing a lot, especially hymns. The added bonus was that I became the home's responsibility for spiritual care. I was given every freedom to conduct services, especially Good Friday, Easter, Harvest, Remembrance Day and Christmas. I was also on the spot for prayer, Bible study and sharing Holy Communion. Frequently I was called upon to comfort the bereaved and officiate at the funerals when loved ones departed.

On this particular freezing cold day we had a very bad hailstorm. As I drove home through the storm, the hailstones were falling like miniature golf balls. I knew that my nephew would be waiting at home for me since he had come to live with my mother and me a few years earlier. The arrangement worked well at the time since my nephew, Adie, short for Adrian, has a mental illness. My mother was physically disabled and found it hard to move around the home. Consequently she cared for Adie and advised him how to do and cope with things. Adie, on the other hand, served as her eyes and her legs and did lots of domestic jobs in and around the home. The combination worked very well.

When my mother died, my sister Audrey, who is Adie's mum, was constantly on hand because she lives next door and was able to pop in regularly. She actually took on the role that Mum had undertaken, especially now that she had become a widow herself.

Well, as I drove into the road where I live, I was met with an alarming sight. There were fire engines, an ambulance, firemen everywhere and a gathering of gawping neighbours gathered outside my house.

There was already a large pile of burning furniture on the lawn. The three-piece suite was reduced to a pile of springs. The television had melted. Bookcases of books and pictures were charred remains. Flames seemed to be everywhere. A loud banging, and breaking of doors, and cracking and breaking of windows, could be heard above the shouting and instructions of the firemen. Then everybody went silent and continued gawping as I arrived on the scene.

My sister and Adie were waiting for me. When I saw them I was relieved to know they were safe. Audrey said she had never been so afraid in all her life as she explained what had happened.

I used to lay the newspaper, kindling wood and coal in the fireplace before I went to work every morning, intending to light it when I came home late in the afternoon.

Adie was usually next door with my sister or in his room during the day whilst I was at work.

On this particular day Adie felt how cold it was. He also saw the hailstones and guessed that I would be cold when I arrived. He thought he would do me a great favour, and light the fire, so that I could come in to some warmth. It was such a lovely thought.

He put a match to the newspaper and kindling wood but he could not get it to burn. Hailstones had come down the chimney, made the firemaking materials very wet, and consequently he could not get the fire to light.

At this point Adie thought of a good idea. He remembered that I keep a gallon of petrol in the garden shed for use in the lawn mower. He also remembered that I had put a small amount in a jam jar, to encourage our Guy Fawkes' bonfire to start the previous year when it was wet. Now he desperately wanted me to come home to a warm room. Unfortunately it turned out to be far warmer than he anticipated; Adie had unscrewed the can of petrol and decided to thrust some of it on to the smouldering wood in the living-room grate. There was a big rush of flame that caught Adie's jumper sleeve alight, so he threw the can into the hearth. In seconds it exploded. The furniture, curtains, books and all my belongings were ablaze. Adie, in a panic, ran next door to alert his mother, shouting, "Mum, the house is on fire!" Audrey rang the fire brigade. The police arrived and phoned for an ambulance, thinking that Adie's burnt arm should receive attention, but he refused to go to hospital. My sister said she had been petrified. It seemed like an eternity whilst they were waiting for the fire brigade to arrive. She was worried that her house would be destroyed too as she lived next door and our houses were semi-detached. In the midst of all the drama and confusion I felt an amazing inner calm. I was so relieved to see that Audrey and Adie were alright and that next door was unscathed. I counted my blessings. I had so much peace, which I knew was from God.

The fire chief said he was amazed at the way I had accepted the tragedy, confessing that if it had happened to him, he would have been utterly devastated.

I simply wanted to get away from all the spectators. The fire chief was flabbergasted when I gathered my sister and nephew together and I drove them off to get a meal at a restaurant.

It took nine months for the house to be sorted out, and I was able to obtain all the necessities before I could return to some semblance of order, and to get rid of the smell of smoke and burning.

The local care authorities took the opportunity to re-access Adie's mental condition. It was decided that it would be beneficial for him to live with only a handful of people in a beautiful care home only a few miles away. He is blissfully happy living there and loves doing housework and gardening and socialising in a magnificent setting.

Knowing that Adie is now in safety, and so well cared for, is a bonus for my sister and myself. Especially when I am away on tour or far distant in the ministry. So the words of Romans 8 verse 28 take on a very special meaning: "And we know that all things work together for good to them that love God, to them who are the called according to His purpose."

Maybe the devil, the old known enemy, may have desired to attack me and the work for the Lord by fire. He failed. Just as when Shadrach, Meshach and Abednego were forced into a fiery furnace. The Lord delivered them. We too were blessed by the blessing and protection of God when He undertook for us as well.

In Genesis Chapter 50 we read how Joseph was badly treated, sold as a slave, falsely accused of rape and imprisoned. God was with him through every experience as He is with us. Joseph, after many trials and difficulties, was able to say, "But as for you, you thought evil against me; but God meant it unto good, to bring to pass, to save much people alive." I do believe that nothing is an accident with God, but He is continually working for our good. God is Love!

Believing that I know the Christ for every crisis, it is such an encouragement and blessing to know that He never leaves or forsakes us. David, the author of the 139th Psalm, recorded, "Whither shall I go from your spirit? Or whither shall I flee from your presence? If I ascend up into heaven, you art there: if I make my bed in hell, behold, you are there." He also said, "Even there shall your hand lead me, and your right hand shall hold me." I proved this very especially when I was on ministry in Kenya.

Taking some time off for sightseeing in Nairobi, I came across what I thought was a large group of boy scouts marching and then forming up doing physical exercises, in a large quadrangle. It was a very colourful display in the centre of a cluster of brick buildings. Typical of a touring tourist, I took some photographs and was immediately seized by two very large men who frog-marched me into the office.

I was instantly interrogated about why I was there, and what I was doing. They refused to believe my story about the boy scouts and insisted that I was taking forbidden photographs of the Kenyan Army. One of the interrogators said I had committed a very serious offence as he removed the film from my camera.

I was taken to a different room and left alone, as the two men who arrested me went to speak to a third individual in another room. I sat there for at least an hour without seeing or hearing anybody.

All of a sudden the door opened, and what looked like a much younger officer put his head around the door. He put two fingers to his lips and whispered the word, "Come!" as he beckoned me to follow him. He opened the door at the end of the passage, thrust me through it and closed it quickly behind me.

In seconds I escaped through a gap in the wall where vehicles drove in and out. I took the opportunity to run a fair distance until I was in a busy street where shoppers were. I was not followed. I wondered how my escape was so possible and so easy. I also wondered how my mysterious disappearance had affected my captors.

A few days later I went on a very long and slow train journey from Nairobi to Mombasa. I enjoyed the scenery and taking in all the wildlife, including the giraffes and lions, looking at the ostriches and birds, including the menacing vultures. A beautiful country. The beach at Mombasa was one of the loveliest beaches I have visited in the world. With its silver sand, warm sea and climate since it is on the Indian Ocean, and exceptionally very kind and generous people.

One afternoon I fell asleep on the hot sand, and when I awoke I went swimming in the sea to cool off. Five minutes later I had a strange stinging sensation in my right foot and I saw the water turning red as my foot was bleeding. I thought

I had been bitten by something, or maybe that I had trodden on some wire or painful object.

I sat on the beach looking at my injured foot and I could see a lot of thorn-like prickles sticking out of it. As I was wondering what to do, I heard a shout, and a young lad came running up to me. I was amazed that he spoke in very good English. Even more amazing was the fact that he looked so similar to the young man who had rescued me from the Kenyan Army barracks.

I was soon to learn that I had trodden on some kind of very poisonous fungus. It could be fatal and it was imperative that the fungus spores should be removed instantly.

The lad produced two large leaves with spiked stems. He used the two spikes as though they were tweezers, one on each side of the prickles, and plucked them, one by one, from the sole of my foot. It took him more than an hour to complete the job to his satisfaction. I had lost quite a lot of blood as the prickles were in deep.

The young man warned me about the area being dangerous and then I realised why so few people were actually in the water.

I very happily rewarded my helper with a monetary gift as he left. Moments later he returned, with a very wide grin, having bought me a cold drink. It seemed like my guardian angel was on duty again.

During one of my world tours I arrived at the airport in Japan to await my next flight to Vancouver. This was one of the more important stops for ministry as I was expected two days later. As soon as I arrived at the terminal in Tokyo I discovered that my last flight for Vancouver had been cancelled. The next departure would not be for a further couple of days.

I stood with my eyes closed in prayer and told God my problem. Almost immediately, a very small Japanese man touched me on the arm. Smiling, he said in perfect English, "Do not be afraid!" I thought it was a strange thing for him to say because I was not afraid but somewhat anxious and frustrated.

"You have a problem?" the little man asked, and I told him the fact that I needed to go to Vancouver that night but there was no flight. The man took my arm and propelled me to the desk, still smiling, and now whispered again, "Don't be afraid." My new little friend spoke to an official behind a desk, who didn't have much to say but listened intently to what he was being told in Japanese. I could not understand a word. The two men chatted for a long time. The official suddenly disappeared and then returned a few moments later with another colleague. Now I was witnessing the three men being deep in conversation. The two officials continued to shake their heads in unison, and as far I could tell, they were saying they could not help. In the meantime my friend was jabbering and raising his voice.

At this point, a third man came on to the scene and, ignoring the other two, he beamed at the little man and me.

"I understand you need to go to Vancouver this evening?" he said, addressing me. "Are you available to leave within the hour?" This sounded very promising and I said I was available from that minute.

"I have received a last-minute cancellation for the next flight to Los Angeles," he explained. "If you take that flight you will be in L.A. and able to get a connecting flight to Vancouver. A few hours late is better than a few days."

There was no extra charge because the airline had

cancelled my original flight and caused me inconvenience. A young lady was then called to the desk to give me different documentation and direct me to the departure lounge.

I knew this would never have been possible without the Lord's intervention. Instantly I thought he had sent another of those guardian angels. I was so grateful for his help and for pleading my cause at the airport. I turned to thank him for all his support and help. I was desperate to give him an offering of thanks for rescuing me at a critical time, but he was nowhere to be seen.

Hebrews 13 verse 2 encourages us to, "Be not forgetful to entertain strangers: for thereby some have entertained angels unawares." I can certainly say, "Amen," to that and to reiterate, "We certainly do have the Christ for every crisis!"

TWENTY-THREE

A couple of days ago I beheld a wonderful sight. As I stopped at our village green to post some letters, a bus bringing children home from school arrived at the local bus stop. I was very happy to see among the children, two young boys, about ten years of age, step off the bus and walked down the road with their arms draped around each other's shoulders. One little boy was very black-skinned and his pal very white-skinned.

The youngsters were laughing and chatting very excitedly as they passed me. They looked as though they didn't have a single care in the whole wide world. They were obviously enjoying each other's company and sharing all things common.

I thought how wonderful it would be if all of us in the world lived together in harmony as those lovely children. A world where race and colour makes no difference whatsoever. The sight of those boys embracing each other reminded me of a little chorus we sang at Sunday school many years ago. It went something like this:

Jesus died for all the children, All the children of the world,

*Red and yellow, black and white, All are precious in
His sight.
Jesus died for all the children of the world.*

Whatever the colour of our skin, it is only a covering.
Precious life-giving crimson blood flows through every vein
of every one of us on the planet. It should make no difference
at all. We are all part of God's creation and He is no respecter
of persons so that we are all equal in His sight.

The children were not showing any differences or
embracing any prejudices. How much God can teach us
through children.

Psalm 127 verse 3 reminds us that, "Children are an
heritage of the Lord: and the fruit of the womb is His reward."
Clearly showing that all are indeed precious in His sight.

On an occasion when Jesus's disciples rebuked parents for
bringing children to Him, St. Mark Chapter 10 tells us that,
"When Jesus saw it, He was much displeased, and said unto
them, Suffer the little children to come unto me, and forbid
them not; for of such is the kingdom of God." So it does not
matter, whether we be young or old, male or female, whatever
the colour of our skin might be, or where we were born, because
we are all part of creation. God loves each one of us as His own.

In my early relationship with the Kray twins, they
introduced me to one of their very special friends – Justin
Fashanu, a son of a Nigerian barrister and his Guyanese
mother. A black boy who grew up to excel both at boxing
and football. There was a time in his early life when he
was struggling to decide on a boxing or football career.
Eventually football won and he started as a seventeen-year-
old apprentice with Norwich City.

Justin loved football and some of his scoring was spectacular. He was sought by Nottingham Forest and was the first black footballer to command a one million-pound transfer fee.

Justin read my book *Road to Nowhere* on the recommendation of Ronnie Kray and became very interested in our Garford Mission Youth Cub. Having obtained my address from the Kray twins, he wrote to say that he would like to meet me and the members of the club. Needless to say our young people were delighted at the prospect of such a celebrity footballer coming to spend an evening with us.

Adrian, our secretary, went with me to meet Justin at Oxford Station, and we took him to a local hotel for a meal before driving him to Garford village.

It was an unforgettable evening. Justin took part in table tennis and various games, posed for photographs, and shared a lot of football tips for our young enthusiasts. At the end of the evening I drove him to friends who had a lovely bed and breakfast guest house in Oxford and he stayed overnight.

Justin was very happy telling me all about his conversion. He was a great believer in prayer but struggled about understanding the Bible. We prayed together and went through some Scriptures that he wanted to understand.

The following morning I drove Justin to his flat in Nottingham. After a snack, I drove him on for training at the Nottingham Forest training ground.

In the two days that we had spent together, I learned a lot about Justin's private life, family and career. He was so frank and opened up about very personal things. His relationship with his family, the fact that he was gay, problems with his manager and mentioned certain things about teammates in various clubs that he had been involved with. He gave me a list of various things he wanted me to pray for.

From that day until he died, Justin wrote and telephoned me regularly to share his problems, struggles, successes and always more requests for prayer.

Justin had a considerable struggle with life which pulled him in three specific directions. He found it difficult to reconcile his Christian life, which was very important to him, with the fact that he was gay. The third dimension was a cloak of secrecy which he was trying to hide from others in the football world. It was a constant battle.

Justin's allegiance to God meant he tried hard every day to witness at being a Christian. However, the draw of the world, and his experiences with tales from other gay friends, led him to explore places, people and pleasures that made him unhappy. He confessed continually that too often his resolve to be strong always ended in weakness.

In spite of the inner turmoil, Justin kept reading and re-reading the Scriptures. He often referred to himself as he read and quoted James Chapter 4: "Submit yourselves therefore to God. Resist the devil, and he will flee from you. Draw near to God, and He will draw near to you. Cleanse your hands, you sinners, and purify your hearts, you double minded." After a brief period of melancholy and depression, Justin pleaded with me to visit him in London.

I discovered that in a time of frustation with himself he had kicked out at a French window and cut his foot quite badly on the broken glass. He was very worried that the wound would affect his footballing for ever. I prayed with him and he received what he called a miracle healing. Even so, it did not detract him from his lifestyle and obsession of meeting celebrities and coming out as gay in a daily newspaper. Sadly coming out as gay had repercussions for Justin. He became the target of constant crowd abuse and certain friends turned against him. The saddest thing in his entire life was that a close family member turned against him also.

Justin and I stayed in touch when he moved around various clubs. I felt his enthusiasm was not the same as it had been. He had so many distractions in his private life. Constant sadness never left him. He felt no longer wanted by some folk that he loved, and disowned by members of his family. Justin suddenly wanted to renew his talents abroad and set his eyes and heart on America. It seemed to me that he was not very happy there either and was always homesick for Britain.

Justin continued to send cards and telephoned me when he had some good news to share, or requesting prayer for something he was worried about. It was mostly the latter. He was desperate for me to pray about his reconciliation with his loved ones.

I never knew about the alleged sexual assault he had committed, or his sudden departure from America and return to Britain.

I was deeply saddened to read in the daily newspapers that Justin had committed suicide in a deserted lock-up garage in London.

The thought that this young man, only thirty-seven years of age, could no longer face the future and the problems of the past, was hard to bear. I often wondered if I could have been more helpful, or understanding, even supportive. These must be the thoughts of many when they are faced by similar circumstances. We say, "If we had only known." But we do not know and there is little we can do in hindsight. I know that Justin never wanted to embarrass his family and friends. I did learn from Justin's death that there must be many desperate souls like him. It has made me so much more aware of this fact, and prompts me always to urge folk to seek professional and practical help. There is always someone, somewhere, on hand to lend a listening ear and to give a helping hand. That is a legacy I received from this dear friend. I commit him to the mercy of the Lord Who in His Word has given us comforting words. Psalm 23 verse 4: "Yea, though I walk through the valley of the shadow of death, I will fear no evil: for Thou art with me; Thy rod and Thy staff they comfort me."

I also appreciated how the Kray twins introduced me to various well-known friends, including the very glamorous actress and film star Diana Dors.

This lovely lady was a very talented actress and a beautiful personality as well. As a young man I saw her films and followed her career. She was born in Swindon, which is less than twenty miles from where I live.

Diana was very impressed when the Krays told her about different answers to prayer when she called during the filming of one of her films in London. Later on when she became unwell she asked for prayers for herself, although she was more worried for her husband, Alan Lake, who appeared to be more concerned about her ill health than she was.

Sadly in May of the following year Diana passed away, having lost her battle with cancer. At the Kray twins' request I picked up flowers and attended her funeral at the Sacred Heart Church at Sunningdale near Ascot in Berkshire.

Alan was never the same after Diana died and said it was as though half of him had died as well. Reggie tried to send him encouragement, but he was constantly sad and, between us, we tried to console Alan the very best as we could, especially for Diana's youngest son Jason's sake.

Five months after Diana Dors' death, Alan committed suicide. This time, my friend Adrian (who helped me bring home the Krays' pigeon trophy from London) accompanied me to Alan's funeral at the same church in Sunningdale. It was virtually the same family and mourners present, including Charlie Kray.

Adrian and I had a brief word with Jason, who was only fifteen, before he left the cemetery with his girlfriend.

I spent so much time praying for Jason as he had lost both of his parents within weeks. It was a blessing to know that he had gone to live with his half-brother, Gary, in California.

The Kray twins were saddened by the fact that Diana Dors and Alan Lake were no longer with us, and that Jason was out of the country, but it did bring Charlie Kray and I closer together. Charlie, at the time of Alan's death, was agonising over Jason's future and mentioned his concern to the twins. However, Jason went on to have a turbulent life, experiencing many highs and just as many lows, so that just a couple of days before his fiftieth birthday he too took his own life as well.

When a father and a son both decide to take their own lives, it is a shock and brings much sadness to family and those who are left behind. Prime Minister Winston Churchill once said, "Who can know the human heart?" I often wondered if he had taken the words from Jeremiah Chapter 17 verse 9: "The heart is deceitful above all things, and desp,.. _..,ly wicked: who can know it?"

In the affairs of the heart, I have seen so many amazing

things in many lives. None more so than the Duke and Duchess of Windsor and Margot Fonteyn and her husband Dr. Roberto Arias.

The Duke of Windsor abdicated the British throne as King Edward the Eighth for Wallis Simpson, the woman he loved. When the Duke and Duchess gave me their royal card, bearing their signatures, for my handwritten copy of the New Testament, I was able to say, "Sir, you have a wonderful story. You abdicated your throne for the lady you love. I have such a story – King Jesus left His throne and the glory of Heaven because He loves me and came to save me when I was lost."

For Dame Margot Fonteyn, the famous ballerina, and her husband Dr. Roberto Arias, it was an amazing union of love which was strengthened by daily heartache and pain.

The way in which God brings us together is very often spectacular, and unlike anything we could ever think or imagine. So it was with my introduction to Margot Fonteyn.

For me it was just another gospel meeting when I was invited to give my Christian testimony at a venue in the north of England.

After the meeting, a very elegant lady who was a ballerina introduced me to her husband, who was very big in the building industry. I could see a very large swelling on his head, and he explained that he was suffering from a massive brain tumour. He asked me to pray for him.

Not very long after our meeting and praying together, the gentleman received a wonderful healing and we kept in touch. He remained on the records at a famous hosptal in London, and he and his wife came to the hospital annually for a check-up. On every visit they invited me to meet them for afternoon tea with them at The Ritz.

It was at one of the meetings at The Ritz that ballerina Dame Alicia Markova joined us for tea. I was enthralled with her reminiscences of her performances, particularly with the way she enthused about dancing in the great classical ballet *Giselle*. I was able to witness to Alicia Markova that I had, by nothing less than a miracle, seen *Giselle* at the Royal Opera House, Covent Garden, when Dame Margot Fonteyn danced with the equally famous Rudolf Nureyev.

Prior to the meeting, Margot had heard about my handwritten New Testament from a technical director. I was invited to meet her at a centre where she was giving lessons. Unfortunately, or so I thought at the time, she fell ill during the week and she sent me a telegram to cancel our meeting. She promised to make another appointment in the future, but some time went by without a word until we got near to Christmas. She just hoped that when I was next in London I would contact her.

I saw that a gala performance of *Giselle* was being staged at the Royal Opera House and I could visit her that day and ask for her at the stage door.

Naturally I applied for a ticket to see *Giselle* but it was impossible. The newspapers reported that the tickets were like gold dust and had been completely sold out well in advance. Furthermore, a crowd of people had brought blankets and sleeping bags to sleep on the pavement outside the Opera House days before the ballet. All in the forlorn hope of buying last-minute cancellations. I saw a very long line of hopefuls still waiting, even though the management was saying there was no hope.

Things were not going well for me either. I did not have a ticket for the performance and zero hope of buying one.

To cap it all, Margot Fonteyn's assistant met at the stage door and, assuming that I had a ticket and that I was going to the performance, said Margot would prefer to see me after the ballet rather than before because she would have more time to look at the book and speak to me then. I agreed to that arrangement but now wondered what I was going to do for the rest of the evening as it was a freezing night in January. I decided to go to a cafe for a warm drink in Covent Garden.

I walked past all the folk still hopefully queuing for tickets as I looked for a cafe. Just as I had passed the end of the queue, and I was going on into the night, I was very suddenly and violently grabbed by a young and breathless lady who was tugging at my arm.

In a foreign accent and very excitable way she exclaimed, "Have you not got a ticket? Speak to me quickly! Do you want my spare ticket?"

No sooner had I said, "No," and, "Yes, I would like one," than she grabbed my hand and we ran together, hand in hand, around the outside of the Opera House and arrived, breathless, inside. Late arrivals have to wait outside until the interval.

Almost immediately we were seated and watching Margot Fonteyn and Rudolf Nureyev dance like I had never seen dancers do before or ever since. It was during the interval that I learnt the young lady's name was Sylvan; she was from Switzerland, and her fiancé had gone down with scarlet fever and was unable to use his ticket. I hoped she was not a carrier of the complaint. I was so happy to give her the money for the ticket and buy her a big box of chocolates as a thank-you present during the interval. We parted with a promise of my prayers for her and the boyfriend, as at the end of the performance she left as quickly as she had arrived. I was duly invited to sit and wait for Margot whilst she got refreshed and changed. As I waited for her, an ambassador with a small entourage arrived with an enormous bunch of roses. The little group looked puzzled as I was invited in first.

Dame Margot loved to talk about her faith and the handwritten New Testament, which she signed with a very large signature. She spoke at length about the assassination attempt on her husband's life which left him paralysed as a quadriplegic. She explained how Dr. Roberto Arias (her husband) was in Stoke Mandeville Hospital near Aylesbury, and how she motored to and fro London regularly to meet him, often very late in the evenings. Then she would return to London for long days of teaching dance or rehearsals before returning to the hospital. She endured this kind of a lifestyle for months with very little rest or sleep. One of the reasons, she explained, was because of very expensive hospital bills.

What a combination of love, care and respect encompassed them both. In her own words Dame Margot said, "I could never do what I do without the love and care of my God, I rely on Him for everything. My life, my strength, my career, just everything."

I needed to keep reminding the lovely lady that the ambassador was still waiting to meet her. We felt as though we could have shared much more about the goodness of God, but we had already spent a long time together. At her request I promised to pray for two of her requests – for her husband and for Rudolf Nureyev.

Again we see the goodness of our God and how He continues to work in amazing ways.

In the first place I had been sad and disappointed that my

meeting with Margot Fonteyn was postponed because of her sickness. God over-ruled! If we had met at that time, I would never have seen Rudolf Nureyev, never seen the miracle of God sending a person with a ticket in an instant, or allowing me in to see *Giselle*, and to choose me from a crowd that had been waiting for days.

I am positive of the fact that I do not deserve so many privileges and benefits which God bestows upon me. I feel unworthy because of the times I sometimes doubt.

Yet, I do believe I have royal privileges and benefits because I am a child of the King of Kings. Psalm 84 verse 11 is a constant reminder that "no good thing will He withhold from them that walk uprightly".

When I think of the rich and famous personalities that I have met through the years, I realise that so many of them are spiritually bankrupt and desperately unhappy. I read recently that thirty-seven millionaires had taken their own lives in a very short period of time. All that glitters is not gold. Often under a sparkling exterior of wealth, glamour and influence, lurks a wide-open void which only God can fill. Meeting the very beautiful actress Elizabeth Taylor after a play, *The Little Foxes*, in London's West End, she told me that God would most certainly have a place in Heaven for her because she was extremely generous in donating large sums of money to a certain hospital. I just said simply, "We cannot buy our way into Heaven or get there by good works. Jesus has said in His Word, St. Matthew Chapter 19 verse 23: 'Verily I say unto you, That a rich man (or woman) shall hardly enter into the kingdom of heaven,' and Ephesians 2 verse 9 declares that it is, 'Not of works, lest any man (or woman) should boast.'"

The lady visibly shivered at the thought and looked grave.

Her only comment was, "Oh, you frighten me." It is incredible how many famous personalities seem to be relying on the money or their talents to get them into heaven. The solemn warning is repeated again in St. John 14 verse 6, where Jesus says, "No man (or woman) cometh unto the Father but by me." It is all dependant upon Him, not what we contribute.

Thomas Gray wrote in his famous "Elegy Written in a Country Churchyard":

The boast of heraldry, The pomp of power,
And all that beauty, and all wealth 'ere gave,
Awaits alike the inevitable hour,
The paths of glory lead but to the grave.

The Bible writes it even more clearly in the last verse of Ecclesiastes: "For God shall bring every work into judgement, with every secret thing, whether it be good, or whether it be evil." It behoves us, therefore, to continue in the path of life which God has planned for us and not depart from it.

This world is not our home; we are only passing through. There is so much better ahead of us if only we take the time and trouble to seek it.

Twenty-four

As I continue to walk in the path of life I know that God becomes more precious to me every day. I can truthfully say that every day with Jesus is better than the day before. His word comes constantly to my mind. I believe it with all my heart and I am led by His mighty counsel. I trust God completely for everything that He has in mind for me. I have faith that He is constantly working for my good, and that He will never leave or forsake me for a moment in this life.

I know there is nothing to fear for the future because my future is in His hands. I look back with praise and thanksgiving to Almighty God for all that He has given me. For all of His understanding, undertaking and bounteous provision. For abundant life, the blessing and companionship of a loving family and very precious friends.

I am grateful for all the teachers of His Word, the fellowship of my Christian brothers and sisters, for encouragement and blessing me in so many ways.

But it is to Almighty God, His loving and Precious Son Who is my Saviour, and to the unction and the Power of His Holy Spirit, that I must need bow my knees in worship, thanksgiving and praise. Without the Father, Son and Holy Spirit I am nothing.

I love walking in the countryside or on some warm and sandy beach. However, there is nothing like walking in the path of life with the Master and walking in His footsteps. As we have travelled along the path we have had some wonderful conversations. We laugh and cry together and find some of the situations that we have encountered to be hilarious. Together we have toiled in the sun, blessings have poured upon our heads like the showers of rain, and when the fog and mist appeared I found it difficult to see where I was going. Thankful, that at those times the Master sees the clear way ahead and leads me on into the unknown.

Sometimes the path is uphill and steep. On occasions the path is full of potholes, mud and puddles, but once they are passed and we journey on, we are happy for all that we have been brought through. The Lord is an amazing travelling companion and friend. Even when night and darkness fall upon us and the need to stop or rest awhile, we have that never-failing assurance that the darkness will be followed by a brand-new day.

Death is the only fact that will tell me that I have come to the end of the path. There is no going on from here. For the Christian traveller we know that death is swallowed up in victory. Why? Because He Who created us, watched over us through every second of our Christian pilgrimage, will be with us at the very end of this earthly journey.

It is for this very moment that the Bible, Psalm 23 verse 4, assures us, "Yes, though I walk through the valley of the shadow of death, I will fear no evil: for Thou art with me; Thy rod and staff they comfort me."

I see death for the Christian to be nothing more than slipping through a shadow. In the twinkling of an eye we shall leave this dark earthly scene, to be immediately in heaven and the Presence of the Lord. All of this because Jesus paid the price.

He took our sins upon Himself when He suffered on the Cross. He taught us that when we repent of sin and acknowledge Him, and thank Him, for paying the price for our salvation through His Precious Blood, we inherit eternal life for Heaven and eternity.

The eternal promise of hope and for the Christian is that "we shall be forever with the Lord". 1 Corinthians 2 verse 9 is a glorious foretaste of what is to come: "As it is written, eye hath not seen, nor ear heard, neither have entered into the heart of man, the things which God hath prepared for them that love Him."

A solemn warning is also given. Hebrews Chapter 9 verse 27: "And as it is appointed unto men once to die, but after this the judgement." Also Roman 5 verse 9: "Much more then, being now justified by His Blood, we shall be saved from wrath through Him." The wrath or the fear of God is not popular teaching but is a very real fact. I hate to think of so many who would opt for a Christ-less eternity.

As in any spirirtual journey, one learns a great deal from sights and experiences, and learns to cope with vast changes and differences along the way. It is often said in life that "one man's meat is another man's poison". Therefore, we often have to adapt, change and adjust our thoughts as we, first and foremost, feel led by God.

Amongst Christians, we sometimes differ in doctrine or interpretation of Scripture. We may have differences of opinion concerning worship or denominational issues, but in my personal view, I feel we should always line up with that which is in accord with the word of God.

Through the decades of walking in my path of spiritual journey, I have been greatly challenged and sometimes severely disciplined by God. I must confess that at such times I have felt embarrassed, hurt and even rebellious. Then I remember that God has said in Isaiah 55, "For my thoughts are not your thoughts, neither are your ways my ways, saith the Lord; For as the heavens are higher than the earth, so are my ways higher than your ways, and my thoughts than your thoughts."

I have learned not to walk by sight but by faith. It can be easy to fall in the trap that Jesus warns us about in St. Matthew 23: "You blind guides, which strain at a gnat, and swallow a camel."

I have, on occasions, shared my thoughts with folk and thought I was speaking the truth in love, when to my surprise I have been severely reprimanded and seemingly caused offence. This worried me very much for years, and I would always seek to apologise for an offence. That was until the Lord showed me that He had used me to speak out and it was not always right for me to apologise.

We know that Jesus caused offence when He spoke the truth in love. St. Matthew 26 verse 21: "Then Jesus said unto them, All you shall be offended because of me this night: for it is written, I will smite the shepherd, and the sheep of the flock shall be scattered abroad."

Many times I have felt very concerned in services and meetings regarding worship. The Oxford Dictionary defines "worship" as "the practice of showing deep respect for and praying to a god or goddess" and "great admiration and respect for someone". I love worship because of the respect and admiration it brings to God.

However, I feel bound to say that some of the "worship" I have experienced, in more than half a century amongst worshippers, has not been worthy of that name.

About worship groups. I was invited to a city church and went along with a Christian couple accompanied by a missionary couple home on furlough. As we went up the steps to the church, we heard the very large sound of over-amplified guitars, drums and cymbals. There was a very strange drumbeat, and it was difficult to hear the words of the songs because of the din of the music.

On arrival at the porch, my missionary friends suddenly froze and clasped each other in their arms. "Oh, no!" they exclaimed together, and the gentleman said, "I do not want to go in." I was amazed when he explained the drum beat was that of tom toms used continually with witch doctors. It was common in Sudan.

My friends asked about the group and how long they had been working together. One of the young girl singers explained that her unconverted boyfriend was the drummer. They had enrolled his help in the hope that he would come under the sound of the gospel and get converted. Can you imagine that being worship?

When I have been invited to preach or give my testimony at various venues throughout Great Britain, invariably we have a time of worship which has gone on for at least an hour before a word has been spoken.

There are several factors which need addressing here, which sadly so many Christians fail to consider. First, almost always, the congregation is asked to stand. This gives very little thought to elderly folk, individuals with painful legs and knees or aching backs. Minutes of standing to praise may be acceptable for some but certainly not for all. As my mother used to say, "I cannot stand very long. I am embarrassed to sit in case people think I don't want to worship." If only the leaders who tell us to stand would also think to tell us when to sit! Praise and worship does not come easy if you are standing in a lot of pain.

Much standing to singing endless choruses and unknown music is a certain turn-off for non-Christians. Especially when it is often too loud, too repetitive, and the words of some amateur chorus writers are most definitely not scriptural.

The Lord looks on our hearts. Is our so-called worship and singing an expression of our love and respect for the ears of God, or do we simply like singing and playing instruments for our pleasure?

One incident about a music group's rendering sticks out in my mind beyond all other. I was invited to preach at an evangelistic meeting in a very large church and a very big congregation. The Presence of the Holy Spirit was keenly felt and I felt a great uplift in my spirit. I just knew that many had been praying for that meeting.

When the invitation was given for anyone wanting to come forward and accept Jesus as Saviour, several came forward from aisle after aisle until there was a long line of seekers at the front of the church.

The music group had been deafening throughout the meeting. As the group of seekers came forward for prayer and counselling, the minister asked the group to play, not sing, something softly. Sadly they didn't seem to understand what softly meant or didn't seem to care. The music was even more deafening.

I could only lip read what the candidates were saying, and they could not hear what I was praying or saying either. No-one made any effort to ask the group to stop or at least to be softer. I had no alternative but to invite the seekers to queue up in the quietness of the porch because it was dark and raining outside. Some folk had wandered off at that point and I knew I had missed some. I am amazed that sometimes Christian folk just cannot see the obvious. Other times I think we fail to see the fact that the devil is wanting to be there with us, or that we are helping him to be made most welcome.

When Joshua and Moses saw how the people sang and worshipped at the golden calf, Joshua said in Exodus 32 verse 18, "It is not the voice of them that shout for mastery, neither is it the voice of them that cry for being overcome; but the noise of them that sing I do hear." Do we ever stop and wonder what God thinks of what we are offering? Is it sweet to His ears or is His hearing diminished by the noise of the singing?

God was present and went past Elijah as he stood in the mountain. 1 Kings 19 explains that, "The Lord was not in the wind, but the Lord was not in the earthquake, the Lord was not in the fire: and after the fire a still small voice." How interesting that God spoke to His servant in a still, small voice. How often have we not heard the still, small voice of God because of the noise of the saints?

A final thought about long sessions of so-called worship and singing. From personal experience I know many speakers at evening meetings, dinners and suppers, feel as I do about lengthy times of music and choruses. So often it takes up so much time that the speaker's time becomes restricted. If the guests are not getting tired from all the food and singing, they are getting anxious about the lateness of the hour.

It is so off-putting when your listeners keep glancing at their watches. It is sad to see folk leave because it has got late and they have to get back home for baby- and children-sitters at home. Some of them may have early starts the next morning. It is such a loss when you get the opportunity to testify for the Lord, and you lose it when the folk get up and leave after so much singing. I am certain that it is for this cause that Jesus said through the gospels of St. Matthew and St. Mark: "For even the Son of man came not to be ministered unto, but to minister, and to give His life a ransom for many."

I often feel for the hotel and venue staff who are waiting to clean up and clear tables before they can go home so late in the evening.

Over and above the little hints I have recorded here for prayerful consideration, it would be failure on my part if I did not write here what the Lord lays on my heart continually.

It is good and right to praise the Lord. The Psalms are especially precious to me and declares that God "inhabits the praises of Israel". But the mistake is, I feel, that we place more emphasis on the praise over and above the preaching of the word or our personal testimony. I repeat what the Lord reminds me endlessly. Psalm 38 verse 2: "For Thou hast magnified Thy Word above all Thy Name."

Let us remember that we have all time and eternity to praise the Lord. It will be endless. No doubt we shall be able to play music and sing and lift up our voices in praise continually. The sobering fact is that we shall not have any opportunity to speak to, to witness or give testimony to the lost ever again. No, not for all eternity. It is for this purpose that we should get our priorities right for God.

In my many conversations with the Lord as we have gone down the path of life, He has reminded me endlessly that His Word is most important. It is not praising, fellowshipping and donating but the preaching of His gospel. Proverbs 11 verse 30 is the best guide: "He that winneth souls is wise."

We need to realise that the Bible has warned us to work as Jesus worked. St. John Chapter 9 verse 2: "I must work the works of Him that sent me, while it is day: for the night cometh, when no man can work."

"Go you therefore, and teach all nations, baptizing them in the Name of the Father, and of the Son, and of the Holy Ghost: Teaching them to observe all things whatsoever I have commanded you: and, lo, I am with you always, even unto the end of the world." We cannot sing souls into Heaven; it is hearing His Word.

I am very conscious of the fact that Jesus says, "Judge not that you be not judged. For with what judgement you judge, you shall be judged," but some obvious things need to be considered. I am conscious that whenever I occupy a pulpit I have a very solemn commitment to the Lord, and I need to respect and hopefully engage with the listeners to His Word. Some grave mistake or omission can have a lasting effect and do no end of harm for the rest of someone's life.

I recall a very embarrassing incident which not only embarrassed two young nurses but had a very detrimental effect on a whole large congregation. Worse still, a short rebuke from the speaker completely quenched the Holy Spirit Presence and working. A very eminent and famous speaker, constantly seen on television, was speaking at a church in the district.

A couple of nurses from one of the Dr. Barnardo's homes were present, but the speaker was speaking far longer than was expected. The nurses were getting anxious because the last bus to town was almost due. They would have to leave the meeting because missing the bus would mean they would be late for their night duty. One of the nurses whispered to her friend, "We must go now or we will miss the bus." Only ten words but it was enough to destroy the evening.

The speaker stopped short in mid-sentence, glared at the nurses and did the unexpected. He actually clicked his fingers, pointed and snapped, "Young lady, please do not speak when I am speaking!" The nurses left and you could hear the drawing in of breath and murmurings from other members of the congregation.

Whenever the man is seen on television or his name mentioned, no-one can recall his talk, but they remember his approach and rebuke to this day.

During His sermon on the mount, Jesus said, "Why, behold you the mote that is in your brother's eye, but consider not the beam that is in your own eye?"

Consequently I remember so many of the gaffes I have made over the years. Some from the pulpit and sometimes from general ministry.

I recall at least two occasions when I have gone to the wrong areas. I have left my hosts wandering around railway stations looking for me when I have been miles away. I was wandering around Rochford when I should have been at Rochester and being sought at Taunton when I was expected at Tiverton.

Once I drove to Worcester, and after a meeting on a very dark night, I was told to follow a couple in their Escort car to their home where I was to stay overnight. I left the church car park and followed the car for about twelve miles. When I drew up beside their car on the drive, a very frightened and bewildered couple got out and asked me what I wanted. I had followed the wrong car. I had to go back to the church car park where my hosts were similarly confused. I found them praying for my return. Thank God it is not He but the devil who is the author of confusion.

A church fellowship in the West Country invited me to take along my handwritten copy of the New Testament. They particularly looked forward to seeing the book and seeing about three hundred famous autographs in it. It had been given considerable publicity. On this occasion I went by train and I had to change at Swindon.

On the second leg of the journey, I realised I had left the special fireproof briefcase containing the Testament on the luggage rack at Swindon. I think that was one of the worst and embarrassing evenings I had ever experienced.

I disappointed the large gathering of people who had come to see the Testament. I was also very anxious and wondering if I would ever see it again. Thankfully I was able to telephone Swindon Station; the Testament was recovered at Weston-Super-Mare and was returned to Swindon, where I collected it the following day.

I am sure that I am not the only preacher who has uttered strange or foolish things from the pulpit. To this day I do not know why I kept referring to Moses going to Pharaoh and telling him to allow the Egyptians to leave Egypt. What I should have said, of course, was the Israelites.

Even a small child challenged me when I was speaking at a Sunday school anniversary. I spoke about Naaman the leper and went into great detail about him and his subsequent healing from leprosy. I explained that the King of Syria wrote a letter of instructions to send to the King of Israel. Then I said, "The King put his letter into an envelope and…?" when, suddenly, a little girl put her hand up in the air. "Excuse me, Sir," she said, "they didn't have envelopes in those days." I feel that it must have been times like these when David wrote, "Out of the mouth of babes and sucklings hast Thou ordained strength," in Psalm 8.

Every year, pre-coronavirus lockdown, I organised various coach trips in the community to transport locals to the seaside or inland events. On one such occasion I wandered into the town and lost my way back to find the coach. Consequently I arrived several minutes late and the driver and all the travellers were waiting for me. I felt so embarrassed when I arrived at the coach to see several faces glued to the windows looking out for me. I was even more embarrassed when I got on the coach and a cheer went up and everyone started clapping. I very much remembered how awkward and out of place I felt, especially several weeks later, when in a church gospel meeting the leader stood at the end of a solo and said, "Now let us give the Lord a clap offering." True to form, everybody clapped because they were told to, which seemed so un-natural and forced. I wonder how the Lord feels after receiving a clap offering?

Our Lord Jesus is the remarkable example of tact and diplomacy. He is the witness to all that we do. He sees the company that we keep as He sends us forth as sheep in the midst of wolves. According to St. Matthew 10 verse 16, Jesus says, "Be you as wise as serpents, and as harmless as doves."

I sometimes wonder why church leaders speak, very often order, congregations to do something which they would not do normally in a place of worship. We are told to give someone a hug or walk around and shake someone's hand and speak, "Peace." Again this takes place because we have received an instruction or commandments from man. This is particularly embarrassing for strangers and visitors and becomes more of a ritual than something that is spontaneous.

When we love the Lord we do not have to be told how to embrace or how to speak to Him. Imagine a man being told by a third party to speak to, kiss or embrace his wife in public. If we love the Lord, His Holy Spirit draws us to Him. The spiritual and natural should always take precedent over given instructions. The Lord looks upon all of our hearts and reminds us often of what He says in St. Matthew Chapter 15 verses 8 and 9: "This people draweth nigh unto me with their mouth, and honoureth me with their lips; but their heart is far from me, But in vain they do worship me, teaching for doctrines the commandments of men." When I think of Jesus's visits to the temple and the synagogue, I try to visualise or imagine how He conducted Himself in the presence of His congregation. Just as important, how do our congregations honour Him?

We must never overlook the very special spiritual needs of all that we worship with. We need each other because, jointly together, we form the body of the church as we are in Christ. The Apostle Paul makes this very clear in 1 Corinthians Chapter 12. He wrote, "For as the body is one, and hath many members, and all the members of that one body, being many, are one body: so also is Christ."

As different parts of our bodies are used for various purposes, so Christians have a diversity of gifts and ministry for the body of Christ and His church. Every person, gift and ministry is usable by and for God. The Apostle listed a few such as apostles, prophets, teachers, miracles and healings. Doubtless we could add many of our own, including hospitality, giving lifts, babysitting, visiting, caring and so on. It is simply a matter or seeing the need and be willing to use the God-given gift.

Not only will this be beneficial for the body but a blessing for those who are on the receiving end of our service.

Most of all, the more we use the body, the more we are a blessing to God. Jesus said, "Verily I say unto you, Inasmuch as you have done it unto one of the least of these my brethren, you have done it unto me." St. Matthew 25 verse 40. We often see the spiritual and physical needs of folk around us, and in our neighbourhoods, but fail to see the very obvious.

I am referring to our elderly and infirm within the community and churches.

We know some of our Christian brothers and sisters have been members and stalwarts of Christian communities for decades. Without many of them, and their faithful witness, doubtless many churches would have floundered to a close years ago. They have been the backbone of the church. Their time and sacrificial giving have been a Godsend and allowed churches to remain open and serving.

In spite of these endearing qualities so many of our senior members are overlooked or ignored. Time and time again, I hear elderly church members complaining that their ministers and administrators "have no time for us anymore. They are only interested in young families". This is a shame and certainly not honouring to God.

Experience through length of time should never be undermined.

A valuable lesson is to be learnt in 1 Kings Chapter 12. King Rehoboam consulted with old men on important matters and they gave him excellent advice. Sadly in verse 8 we read "but he forsook the counsel of the old men, which they had given him, and consulted with the young men" which brought serious repercussions and failure. Prayer and Holy Spirit guidance is always essential in these matters.

Finally, I often feel sad when I see and hear sad comments from some of the Lord's beloved. As far as He is concerned we are equal in His sight. He hath loved us all with everlasting love and the redeemed are all members of His Royal Family. In spite of this, sadly, some members of the family seem to make exceptions and prefer to love, accept and welcome a favoured few.

I would put our bereaved Christian friends at the top of the list.

Some time ago I met up with a Christian brother I had not seen for about ten years. I learnt from him that his dear wife had gone off to be with the Lord shortly after our last meeting. After about five years this friend met and married again. I was very surprised when he said, "It is lovely to be married again because we get invited out together again."

When I asked the friend to explain he told me a very sad story. Apparently during their marriage, the couple were constantly invited out for meals with friends, coach trips and various functions. However, when the wife died, the man was no longer invited at a time when he was very sad and lonely. The strange thing was, when he re-married the social scene seemed to open up again.

It is curious but a fact that couples are far more acceptable than someone on their own. As a never married man, I constantly experience being left out at functions.

On the occasion that I receive an official invitation to a wedding or party I nearly always decline unless I know the hosts very well. It can be a lonely experience to be thrust amongst strangers or put yourself forward for conversation. The few invitations I have receive are mostly exclusive for me. An invitation for "Ken plus one" or "plus friend" could make such a difference. This must sound as though I am canvassing for some invitations, but nothing could be further from the truth. I am very happy as I am. Having had decades of fellowship with Christians wherever I have been away on ministry has been a bonus I admit it is quite different when I am at home. I very seldom hear about any special meetings or events in my area. For me to be invited to preach or testify in a fifteen-mile area of my home would be nothing less than a miracle. I can well understand what Jesus meant when He said in St. Matthew 13 verse 57, "A prophet is not without honour, save in his own country, and in his own house (or district)."

Thinking about Jesus and the Apostle Paul being unmarried too, I wonder if they ever felt overlooked or neglected. It causes me to think on Jesus's words in St. Luke Chapter 9: "Foxes have holes, and birds of the air have nest; but the Son of man hath nowhere to lay His head." Paul was also able to say in 2 Timothy Chapter 4, "No man stood with me, but all men forsook me; I pray God that it may not be laid to their charge." Do we fail to see the needs of others?

In nearly all walks of life there are endless courses, seminars, advances and retreats, programmes and teachings, to learn or further our expertise and efficiency in any given employment or career. There is so much emphasis on computers, Google, Facebook and so on to gather information so we can improve ourselves and information. Practical support and encouragement is constantly sought in every area of life. Without Holy Writ, the Scriptures guided by the Holy Spirit, we flounder on doing the best we can in the hope that it will suit or be beneficial to God.

My prayer is that the contents of this chapter may encourage folk to pause, consider some of the points mentioned and perhaps learn from errors or misunderstandings. It has taken sixty years for me to reach this point on the path of life. I have learnt from many mistakes and learned from wonderful revelations because of the teaching from 2 Timothy Chapter 2 verses 14 and 15: "Of these things put them in remembrance, charging them before the Lord that they strive not about words to no profit, but to the subverting of the hearers. Study to show yourself approved unto God, a workman that needeth not to be ashamed, rightly dividing the word of truth."

TWENTY-FIVE

Without a sense of humour any pastor would be well out of his, or her, depth in the pulpit and community. I readily confess that there have been occasions and moments when I have dissolved into laughter when it has been quite unseemly both in ministry and in public.

Friends and family continually recall some of my most hilarious moments whilst walking in the path of life. After the previous sombre chapter of mistakes and regrets, it is good to lighten the mood with some tales that will cause my reader to smile and relive some of my most embarrassing but entertaining episodes.

As the pastor of a village chapel I was invited to officiate at a wedding. The bride-to-be was most insistent on having the wedding march played on the organ as she came down the aisle. She sang "Here Comes the Bride" at the top of her voice as she came for a rehearsal, as though I needed to be reminded of the tune.

The evening prior to the wedding, the organist phoned to say he was too ill to attend, and so at the last moment I was left without music. Fortunately no hymns were wanted but the wedding march was deemed to be essential.

At 10pm the night before the wedding I had, what I

thought, was a very bright idea. I decided to play the request on my organ at home and to record it on a tape recorder to be played as the bride arrived for the wedding. With no other organist available, and I could not be in two places at the same time, I had hit on the remedy. I stood at the front of the chapel with the bridergroom and his best man. As the bride appeared in the doorway accompanied by her bridesmaids, I nodded to a friend to switch on the tape recorder with the wedding march.

Out bellowed the march with "Here comes the bride… *bong!* All dressed in light… *bong!*" The congregation only sniggered, but to my shame, I burst out laughing and found it difficult to stop. It was not until that moment I realised that when I had recorded the wedding march on the organ the night before, I failed to notice that my Westminster clock struck ten times for ten o'clock. It was all there for everyone to hear: *bong* after *bong* after *bong*. All ten times! Fortunately the wedding party saw the funny side and the congregation had a laugh.

One day I was invited by a young soldier and his wife, who I worked with at the Ministry of Defence, to Christen their baby at our chapel.

The mother's family agreed to come from Bournemouth and the father's from Doncaster. The Christening was scheduled at 2pm because both families had a long way to travel. At almost 3pm there was no sign of the family from Doncaster so those who were present insisted that I continue with the ceremony without the father's family, minus two expected Godparents.

Just as we came to the end of the service the father's family arrived. They had been stuck in a traffic jam for a very long time. They were so sad and disappointed that they had missed the Christening.

There was an urgent discussion between the two families, and the now apparent missing Godparents, so I was asked if I could start again and re-Christen the baby.

Now I am a great believer in the Word. 1 Corinthians Chapter 9 verse 22: "I am made all things to all men, that I might by all means save some." So, I agreed to the families' request. I simply said, "Right, we will call that the rehearsal. Now we shall have the real thing!" The baby was duly dedicated to the Lord, albeit they called it a "Christening", and everybody left happy and satisfied.

I should listen to the advice "never work with children and animals", but once when I was put on the spot, I could not have envisaged what I was put through from a little boy aged about four.

I was the speaker at a very large gathering in Wales that had been organised by the local Corps of the Salvation Army.

When the captain and I went onto the stage we were surprised to find such a large gathering of folk present. There was also a large number of children in the congregation.

The captain whispered in my ear about the children being present. He said he would open the meeting with a hymn, and after it, he suggested I should have something for the children. My mind was working overtime during the singing of the hymn and I decided to tell the story of the prodigal son.

After telling the story, I asked the children if anyone would like to answer any questions about it? A little lad, looking like an inflated teddy bear as he sat in the front row, decked out in his furry overcoat, shouted, "Me!" as he threw his arms up in the air.

I invited the lad on to the stage and lifted him up on to a chair so that we were approximately the same height. I retold the story about the prodigal son with subsequent questions. Each question was answered by the little boy in the most beautiful lyrical Welsh accent.

"Was the father pleased to see the son when he came home?" I asked.

"Yes," he replied, and nodded profusely.

"What did the father give him?"

"Presents!"

"What presents?"

"He gave him the best coat to wear."

I encouraged my young friend to continue so I asked, "Did the father give the young man any other presents?"

There was a silence before the lad answered. "I cannot remember what they were," he volunteered, so with a little bit of prompting I asked, "What did the father give the son to put on his feet?"

Without any further prompting he said, "Shoes," but when asked what the third present was, he had not got a clue. His little face screwed up tight and he closed his eyes, but no sound escaped his lips.

To be of further assistance I tried to jog his memory. I put my hand close to his face and started twiddling my ring round and round my finger. This brought no response at all. So I made it even more noticeable by tapping the ring with one of my fingers.

My young friend began to look decidedly unhappy as he could not recall the third fatherly gift. Desperate to help him, I continued to twiddle my ring and said, "What does a man give a lady when they get married?"

He threw his arms in the air. A smile lit up his little face and he declared at the top of his voice, "*A baby!*"

I just laughed loud and long and was unstoppable. The look of triumph on that cute face was a joy to behold. The congregation laughed but only for a short time. As for me, every time I looked at the child it started me off again.

I have had more than my fair share of embarrassing moments on public ministry. One morning when I arrived at an Army Defence Academy, I was welcomed at the top of a flight of steps by the high-ranking officer commandant. As he stretched out his hand to shake hands with me, I slipped on the icy steps and pulled him down on his knees. He was unsmiling and made no comment when I apologised. It did, however, remind me of David's lament over Saul and Jonathan, his son, as is recorded in the second book of Samuel, Chapter 1 verse 19: "How are the mighty fallen!"

Then there was a time in my early ministry when I taught a young man, Terry, to drive. Whenever I went afield to preach I would take this young protege with me for driving experience.

One very wet summer evening, when we were on our way to a little village chapel in Wiltshire, part of the car exhaust pipe fell off. Gallant Terry retrieved the broken pipe and threw it into the boot, insisting that it would be better for him to get out in the rain to make the recovery of the part rather than me appear like a drowned rat in the pulpit later on. The noise from the car was deafening without the pipe and silencer, but Terry was unperturbed as he drove us to the venue.

The steward of the chapel stood outside the building beneath a very large umbrella and intimated that we should park on a very small lawn adjacent to it. I quickly whispered to Terry. "We will make a quick exit after the service," then suggested, "We need to be first out and get away before the congregation comes out to witness how noisy our car is."

Everything went well and according to plan. We did make a quick exit from the chapel at the end of the service. We ran to the car and climbed in, with Terry in the driving seat. He put his foot down hard on the acceleator for our quick departure, but we had not reckoned with the sodden turf where we had parked.

The wheels spun, but we were not budging but sinking in the lawn. At this point the congregation started to appear and we heard the steward say, "Our brothers are stuck, come on, folk, come and help us. Let us give them a push."

A group of men and women got behind and put their shoulders against the back of the car and braced themselves. No sooner was the word "Push!" heard than Terry put his foot down on the gas. With a deafening roar from the absent silencer and a shoot forward from the vehicle, I looked behind and saw a very sad sight.

A lady beautifully dressed in a summer pink coat and picture hat was covered in thick mud from head to feet. She, along with others from the rescue party, had been on the receiving end of the mud that splattered from the spinning tyres.

When I got home I wrote a letter of apology, but I never received a reply. Not surprisingly I was never invited there again.

Similarly, a young man contacted me from a village near Banbury. His name is Robin and we have been friends for many years.

Robin and the minister of his local village chapel knew of my involvement with my Christian youth work at Garford. They felt God was leading them to introduce some kind of similar Christian work in their village. I was invited along in an advisory capacity and to help out for six weeks. I stayed for about ten years because I just loved working with Robin and being involved with all he did in ministry and leadership in the club.

One evening I got too near to a very deep ditch whilst driving when it was very dark. To my horror I plunged face down into the ditch and got stuck. As Robin and I discussed ways of rescue, a man suddenly appeared from the local fish and chip shop and came up to where we were standing.

Almost without a word, he got into the ditch and lifted the car back on to the road. We had never seen anything like it. A grip, a heave and finally a grunt, and the man had lifted my car back on to firm ground single-handedly. We agreed that if God had not sent us one of His angels on that occasion, He must have had a local man in the vicinity with the strength of Samson. In any event there was not a bit of damage to the car and I was able to drive the thirty miles home without any problems. God is good!

I am indebted to God for so many "incidents" and "close encounters" that He has miraculously protected me from. One very tense but hilarious evening was when I was driving home from Swindon after a missionary evening.

It was mid-winter and a very dark and foggy evening. When I was miles from anywhere, I was driving up a very steep hill when I was overtaken by a small car which braked suddenly in front of me and stopped in the middle of the road. I could not overtake the car and was forced to stop. I was suddenly surrounded by four young lads who were very intimidating and menacing.

I wound down my window, thinking it unwise to step out of the car, as I was ordered to do so by a very mouthy individual. The trio with him all began talking at once as they asked me for cigarettes and money. I told them I did not smoke and tried to stall for time in the hope that another vehicle would pass that way. It was such a bad night and so lonely a place that there was nothing in the vicinity. I only had time to pray quickly and silently: "Lord, please help me!"

"Get out of the car," I was ordered by another of the group. I refused and hoped that I was sounding a lot braver than I felt. Then, it was just as though I was speaking in a voice that was not my own. It was very similar to the very first time that the Lord told me to take the handwritten New Testament to Royalty and heads of state and hundreds of others for His Namesake. That first time God spoke to me through St. Matthew Chapter 10: "But when they deliver you up, take no thought how or what you shall speak: for it shall be given you in that same hour what you shall speak. For it is not you that speak, but the Spirit of your Father which speaketh in you."

I suddenly lost all sense of fear but received a very strong and controlled voice. "You don't frighten me," I began as I leaned out of the car window. "I am a member of the Kray family and we don't get frightened."

The statement was short but electric. The looks on the youths' faces were instantly incredulous and they stared at me with open mouths. Then, almost all together, they went quiet and then started to chatter over each other with questions and observations.

The group asked if I was telling the truth and they peered

through my car window. I pointed at my Bible and the very big handwritten Testament on the passanger seat. Without a further word, I opened the Testament and showed them some of the signatures in it. I was sure to show them the autographs of my "brothers" Charlie, and Ronnie and Reggie Kray. I also mentioned other famous names that I had met and had their signatures there to prove it.

In retrospect, I guess it was a foolish thing to do. What if they had snatched the very valuable book and took off with it? Then I remember God is in control.

What started off as an ambush and a nasty confrontation suddenly became an Evangelistic meeting. The lads listened to every word and asked very searching questions. They were obviously very impressed to know that they were in the presence of a member of the "Kray" family when I explained that I was their "brother" Kenny.

Without any further ado the leader of the gang apologised to me and proffered his hand.

"Sorry, mate!" he exclaimed. "We don't mean any offence."

"None taken," I replied.

"Sorry!" was echoed by the other three lads.

One muttered, "We were only mucking about," by way of an apology, but I knew that they had been earnestly intending to get up to some evil.

I endeavoured to hide a smile as ceremoniously all the lads shook my hand, and with further apologies, they returned to the car and roared off into the night.

Moments later I saw them going into a village pub as I drove past.

I imagined the tale they would tell the customers that they had just been talking to one of the Kray brothers.

No doubt their hearers rubbished their story, as older folk would undoubtedly know that there were only three brothers. Therefore, I am convinced that God does have a fine sense of humour because I remembered how brother Charlie Kray had invited me to become their "adopted Kray brother" when they invited me to the party on the Thames years earlier. I did accept, but I never realised how the Lord would use that unexpected event to be used to my advantage when I had been ambushed and the brothers were no longer with us.

Life as a Christian is never dull. I believe that every day with Jesus is better than the day before. The words of Psalm 118 verse 24 come readily to mind: "This is the day which the Lord hath made; we will rejoice and be glad in it."

Twenty-six

Journeying on in the path of life I am aware of four very different but specific areas of which I must speak. This because of a challenge from God in the reading of Hebrews Chapter 12 verses 12 and 13: "Wherefore lift up the hands which hang down, and the feeble knees; And make straight paths for your feet, lest that which is lame be turned out of the way; and let it rather be healed."

For a long time I have been convinced that many of us Christians have become lame whilst walking in the path of life. This causes us to stumble, become unsteady on our feet and sometimes insecure. It is so easy to lose our way.

The four areas of concern are healing, deliverance, prophecy and speaking in tongues.

I am not an expert by any means in these important topics, but after a great deal of prayer and personal observations and experiences, I have studied the Word at God's Throne of Grace and come to the following conclusions.

I have no wish of taking any Scripture out of context. 2 Timothy Chapter 3 makes it plain: "All scripture is given by inspiration of God, and is profitable for doctrine, for repoof, for correction, for instruction in righteousness: that the man of God may be perfect, thoroughly furnished unto all good works."

I have already written at some length about healings that I have witnessed, but I do feel some further comments might prove to be useful.

Why is it that some people are healed after prayer and some are not? There is no simple answer and I certainly do not know why. I have seen numerous incidents when God has answered miraculous prayers. Some prayers have been answered immediately on the spot, others after a period of time and sometimes there have not appeared to be any sign of healing at all and sometimes they have died. Genesis Chapter 18 verse 25: "Shall not the Judge of all the earth do right?"

I have mentioned before that we do not tell God what to do with regard to healing or any other thing. The well tried and tested formula is "ask", not to dictate. It is important to pray in faith and expectation of a good miraculous answer. God is in the miracle-working business. Expect great things of a great God.

God often is accused of sending illness, pain and some suffering because of sin or by way of punishment. This is not Biblical and this is not in His Divine Nature.

The Apostle Paul had a medical problem which he took to God in prayer, describing it as a "thorn in the flesh". In 2 Corinthians Chapter 12 verses 7 to 9, Paul went on to say, "For this thing I sought the Lord three times that it might depart from me," but there was no change concerning Paul's problem and God answered by saying, "My grace is sufficient for you, for my strength is made perfect in weakness."

Paul realised that although he had no healing from the condition, God had recompensed him with added grace and strength. I am confident that is an answer from God for many of our prayers. He constantly knows our struggles and is a very present help in times of trouble and sickness.

Paul's response was, "Most gladly therefore will I rather glory in my infirmities, that the power of Christ may rest upon me." He recognised that healing and blessings lies ahead for the Christian because according to Psalm 30 verse 5 "weeping may endure for a night, but joy cometh in the morning".

In a coming day, and in Heaven, the words of Revelation Chapter 2 verse 4 will be a reality: "And God shall wipe away all tears from their eyes; and there shall be no more death, neither sorrow, nor crying, neither shall there be any more pain: for the former things are passed away."

Once when I visited a certain church the pastor announced that one of the members was in a great deal of pain. He urged the small congregation to join with him in placing their hands on the victim and praying over him for healing. However, the individual was most emphatic that he did not want this and was clearly embarrassed that he had become the centre of attention.

Undeterred, all the group, except myself, proceeded to lay hands on him and prayed. After the service a few folk asked me why I had not prayed with them and looked stunned when I said it was unscriptural. I explained two things. In James Chapter 4, a question and advice is given in verse 14: "Is any sick among you? Let him call for the elders of the church; and let them pray over him, anointing him in the name of the Lord." In this latest gathering the individual did not call for the elders of the church but very clearly made it plain that he was not seeking prayer. It is a sin to be presumptuous. All that was achieved was that a brother was humiliated and embarrassed.

Later that week the gentleman asked a visiting couple to pray for him and he was in fact healed within days. I felt God was being very gracious in proving a point.

Some time ago I was in the presence of a lady who was giving her testimony at an after-church fellowship meeting. She spoke at length about her success in business and the wonderful ways that she heals and delivers people who are demon-possessed, along with all the plans she was making in speaking in tongues and for her future.

Her talk was very well received with several "Amens" uttered from her listeners. Sitting beside the lady whilst we had refreshments afterwards, I asked her how long she had been a Christian, to which she replied, "All my life!"

She had no idea what I was talking about when I asked her if she had been "born again" and when I mentioned repentance of sin and accepting Christ as her saviour she looked completely bewildered. She had no idea what I was talking about. I am not usually easily shocked, but I must confess that I was not ready for her next statement.

"I am doing an Alpha Course about Christianity," she explained. "I have missed a couple of sessions but I know enough to be qualified in the gifts."

Now I am a great believer in "Judge not, that you be not judged" but I feel it is not judging when you see the obvious. It has well been said, "A little knowledge is a dangerous thing," and more so a tragedy when so-called knowledge transfers to so-called experience. All that glitters is not gold.

A word must be said about evil spirits and demons and possession.

First of all, I do get very concerned when I am in the presence of certain friends who are constantly talking about the devil and evil. We know only too well how both are so clearly evident on every side. Daily we are very conscious of evil activity and the need to be aware and prepared and protected. Indeed, Jesus warned us to pray, "And lead us not into temptation, but deliver us from all evil," in the prayer that He taught us Himself.

It is one thing to be conscious of the devil's endeavours to trick, tempt and deceive us, but it is another thing to have it constantly thrust down out throats from fellow Christians.

I have friends who talk so much of the devil, who widely publicise and advertise his antics, than they ever speak, witness to or to give praise to Father, Son and Holy Spirit. I am sure that the evil one must really revel in the publicity he receives and rejoices that he is seemingly so popular and active. If only we could give as much time and energy to sharing our faith and spreading the gospel.

Going one step further is the growing tendency of administering deliverance from so-called demon possession and evil practices. I am sure many of us have witnessed manifestations that do more harm and danger than good. It certainly should not be practised by anyone who is not positive in what they are doing, or skilled in the moving of the Holy Spirit in such matters. It is better to leave well alone rather than dabble in the unknown.

Why do I say this?

I was in the presence of a Christian gentleman who never ceased emphasising that someone or other was "demon-possessed" or that he had been actively delivering someone from some evil spirit on almost a daily basis. The man was kind to explain how we are to do it and approached an individual to demonstrate. In fairness, he did explain to the individual what he was going to do.

Approaching his friend, he started clapping and shouting, "Get out," at the top of his voice, naming all manner of sins and devils for quite a long time. The shouting and clapping got increasingly louder, so one might suggest that devils and demons are deaf?

After some time the subject let out a sigh of relief and smiled. A murmur of approval and praise went through the entire group. The "deliverer" rubbed his hands together as though he had tossed the offending spirit into the air and, declaring that it was now gone, his subject had been released and delivered.

I will never forget the look on the deliverer's face when I asked, "Where has the demon or the spirit gone?" Seemingly that was something my colleague had not thought about or considered. I could see the blank look on his face. As far as he was concerned he had prayed the spirit out and his work was finished.

With some concern I asked the colleague how he felt about what Jesus said in St. Matthew Chapter 12 verse 43: "When the unclean spirit is gone out of a man, he walketh through dry places, seeking rest, and findeth none. Then he says, I will return to my house (or person) from whence I came out: and when he is come, he findeth it empty, swept, and garnished. Then goeth he, and taketh with himself seven other spirits more wicked than himself, and they enter in and dwell there: and the last state of that man is worse than the first. Even so shall it be in this wicked generation."

How serious is that? A drawn-out or delivered demon spirit can go off to collect and return with seven more evil spirits which are more evil than himself. Imagine having eight indwelling evil spirits instead of one. Only because the well-meaning deliverer called out a spirit but failed to bind it so that it could not return. Very possible to reenter the person that had commanded it to go in the first place.

One could write an entire thesis on the binding of demons, but I believe when God calls someone to that particular ministry, He gives the tools to do the job. Speaking personally, I accept the binding of the spirits is just as important, if not more so, than the deliverance of them. I commit them in Jesus's Name to be chained and cast into a pit from when they may never be allowed to depart from it. Prayer with the Spirit Authority and pleading the covering of the Blood of Christ is absolutely essential.

These things follow the Biblical example of "much prayer and fasting". It is well to remember Whose we are and Whom we serve in light of Ephesians 2 verse 10: "For we are His workmanship, created in Christ Jesus unto good works, which God hath before ordained that we should walk in them."

Sharing my thoughts concerning the healing of the sick and deliverance from evil spirits, etcetera, I am also concerned about Bible prophecy. There seems to be an abundance of folk who insist that they are called of God to be a prophet. They believe they are called of God to teach people of His intentions. People who are convinced that they can predict the future and claim amazing things in advance.

In my own personal experience I have had endless persons sharing with me their prophecies concerning myself.

Almost in every instance I have been assured by the "prophet" that he or she has been, "Given me a special word (or prophecy) from the Lord for you." Or they usually say, "The Lord has told me so and so…" I listen carefully and take it seriously just in case the Lord really has sent me a very important message via this friend. I always return to God in prayer for Him to make His Will and reason known to and for me.

Invariably over the past six decades I doubt that six real prophecies have come to pass for me. How can I explain that? It leaves me wondering who my prophet friends are listening to? I have come to two conclusions. Either they have been listening to some other voice than the Lord's or the Lord has told them a lie, and that would be most cruel and confusing for me. Naturally I know, without any doubt, it is the former because the second alternative is completely impossible. It is quite apart from such a loving and precious Heavenly Father's love and care because of the truth of the Word of God. 2 Timothy 4 verse 3: "The time will come when they will not endure sound doctrine: but after their own lusts shall they heap to themselves teachers, having itching ears; and they shall turn away their ears from the truth, and shall be turned unto fables."

1 Corinthians 14 verse 33 makes it very plain: "For God is not the author of confusion." Sadly too there are many teachers that insist, "That with God all things are possible," which is quite untrue because Hebrews 6 verse 18 states: "It was impossible for God to lie."

Early in my secular Ministry of Defence career I led a series of Bible studies for army officers and other ranks through "Christian Endeavour", and it was a joy to lead members to know the Lord.

Constantly I received "prophecies" from the staff and

other Christian friends that the Lord was going to call me out from the secular work. He was going to give me a wider full-time ministry to the military and, through me, He would evangelise through barracks, units and nations. The result? I retired after forty years of service with the Ministry of Defence in the same location.

A local church had a sudden influx of visitors and swelled the congregation in just over a year. Several prophecies were given concerning this. God had said that He was going to overflow the church that there would not be room enough to gather them all. God would enlarge the church and congregation, and we should expect folk visiting us by the coach-load.

Within four years the congregation dwindled and was divided. Eventually the church closed and was sold. Today a supermarket sits on the site.

Whose voice are those prophets listening to? Who can so blatantly claim they have a message from God? More so, it is increasingly sad that such people continue to claim prophetic ministry when they have already got it so wrong in the past?

It will never cease because this is made plain in Jeremiah 5 verse 31: "The prophets prophesy falsely, and the priests bear rule by their means; and my people love it so." People get hooked on prophecies and love it even when they do not come to pass. It does not stop them eagerly seeking further prophecies.

I know friends who have been unhappy with me when I have not been over-enthusiastic about the messages they have got from God for me. I have listened and prayed and sought God's will in those instances. It is essential to prove what God is intimating.

As I see it, I have been talking with God for the past sixty years plus. He has shown me amazing things, answered endless prayers, performed numerous miracles; why, therefore, would He choose to send me a prophetic message via a third party when we are on daily speaking terms?

Finally I choose to make some comment on the subject of "speaking in tongues". I must confess that I did not really understand what this meant. Many years ago I was attending meetings and services where such a "holy language" was being spoken regularly, but I could not understand a word. I was very concerned about this because it seemed to be coming more and more popular in churches, but I did not feel a part of it. I was convinced that I was missing out on something very important.

I mentioned this to several Christian friends at the time. In almost every instance they insisted that I was missing out on a totally special Holy Spirit experience, that I was only offering God praise in part and that I needed to seek the "baptism of the Holy Spirit".

Over one weekend I promised God and myself that I was going to earnestly seek the gift of speaking in tongues.

I went over my favourite fields in solitude and prayed very earnestly. I pleaded with God that He would not allow me to go home without this new experience which I totally and urgently desired.

I remember it was midsummer and the fields were aglow with golden buttercups, and then suddenly, without any warning whatsoever, I found my tongue went loose and I heard strange sounds coming out of my mouth. It would not cease even when I tried to stop it.

I thought, this is it! I was convinced that I was now

speaking in tongues and I felt light-headed and started to stagger. I felt that this was the real thing because I really did feel as though I was reeling as though I was drunk. As far as I was convinced, the experience was similar to what the disciples experienced at Pentecost. All the people that were present, (according to Acts Chapter 2) said, "What meaneth this?"

Others, mocking, said, "These men are full of new wine." That was exactly how I felt. The Apostle stood before the crowd and said, "These are not drunken, as you suppose, seeking it is but the third hour of the day."

By the time I reached home I had a headache and, absolutely unlike me, I felt very quiet, lifeless and quite depressed. It was really quite foreign to anything I had before, and I lost any further enthusiam to seek the experience again. The Lord knows my heart.

It took several months of prayer and Bible study before I was finally convinced that "speaking in tongues" was not for me. When I am the only person not so speaking in a group it does not bother me anymore.

I could not find any reference about "being baptized in the Holy Spirit" in any Scripture. The nearest thing I read was in St. Matthew 3, when John the Baptist said, "I indeed baptize you with water unto repentance: but He (Jesus) that cometh after me is mightier than I... He shall baptize you with the Holy Ghost." There is no evidence of John the Baptist speaking in tongues but great emphasis on sharing the gospel message and winning souls for Christ.

Then in Acts Chapter 2, on the day of Pentecost, it seems to me, that the apostles were endued with Holy Spirit Power to speak languages they had never learned so that sixteen different nationalities could hear the gospel in their own language.

Consequently three thousand precious souls were converted.

As far as I am concerned, the importance is not in the speaking of tongues but the saving of the precious souls. The tongues were a means to that end.

I think it important to say that in all my experiences of hearing folk speaking in tongues, I have never heard a specific language spoken but a kind of babbling with repetitions which would most certainly require an interpreter at each session. I have never once heard a word that I have understood.

The Apostle Paul made it clear that no tongues should be used except when the people could understand. He makes this very clear in 1 Corinthians 14 verses 27 and 28: "If any man speak in an unknown tongue, let it be by two, or at the most by three, and that by course; and let one interpret. But if there be no interpreter, let him keep silence in the church; and let him speak unto himself, and to God."

I am encouraged by Paul, who also said in the same chapter, "I thank my God, I speak with tongues more than you all: Yet in the church I had rather speak five words with my understanding, that by my voice I might teach others also, than ten thousand words in an unknown tongue." I can say a hearty "Amen" to that.

I often think of an amusing experience I witnessed in a city church many years ago. Sitting in the congregation I heard a man "speaking in tongues" in a pew a couple of rows behind me. As soon as the prayer ceased an interpreter got up and delivered the interpretation. It was all about what God was doing and greater things that He was going to do. From the murmuring and amens it was all readily accepted.

At the end of the meeting, the elder stood in the doorway of the church, shaking hands with the congregation. He gripped the proffered hand of the man who had spoken the tongue and said, "It was good to have you with us this morning, brother. Thank you for bringing us that tongue." The smile suddenly disappeared from the interpreter's face when the visitor smiled and said, "I wasn't speaking in tongues but simply in Welsh. I am from Wales, you see. I have to say that what you interpreted was not by any means what I prayed."

Perhaps I have not missed out on too much by not listening to other tongues!

I have passed many trees and walked through many ferns and flowers with Jesus whilst walking through this Path of Life with Him. He has always made His plan and will clearly known to me. I have never needed a substitute or interpreter.

"The Lord is my Shepherd; I shall not want. He that enters in by the door is the shepherd of the sheep. And when he puts forth his own sheep, he goes before them, and the sheep follow him: for they know his voice. And a stranger will they not follow, but will flee from him: for they know not the voice of strangers." We do well to know the difference.

Twenty-seven

I am now a man of riper years, but I still very much enjoy wandering through leafy woods or down country paths. I love to trample through grassy fields and brush against a host of colourful wildflowers: buttercups, primroses and forests blue with bluebells. With the sun shining brightly from almost a cloudless sky one can see for miles. Hills in the distance, a winding brook, gated fields and dusty paths.

There is so much to see of God's wonderful creation if we just take the time to observe it. How good it is to take in the warmth of the sun. What a joy to behold the mooing of cows in the field, bleating sheep munching at the grass. Maybe a squirrel scurrying from a tree or a surprise appearance of a fox or a badger. Birds flying heavenwards and more sedate earth-bound pheasants and partridges wandering at will. The joy of breathing in God's fresh air, and the tranquillity and peace, brings a real sense of joy. It seems as though all creation is echoing Scripture. "This is the Lord's doing; it is marvellous in our eyes. This is the day which the Lord hath made; we will rejoice and be glad in it."

But what a difference a day can make.

After a brilliant yesterday we now encounter quite a new and different day today. Today we have a dark grey sky and pouring rain. Blustery winds and cold air all around. The flowers look sodden; even the cattle and birds are looking soaked. The dusty path has made us cautious as we manoeuvre around deep mud and puddles. With the wetness of the weather we feel damp and decidedly uncomfortable. Even our attitude has changed. Instead of enjoying the beauty of the country on every side, we will probably be hurrying our footsteps, wrapping some protective clothing about us, dodging the raindrops falling from the trees and heading as fast as we can to some form of shelter.

Even Scripture speaks of walking in different paths. David in the Psalms reminds us of the following:

> *Teach me Your way, O Lord, and lead me again in a plain path.*
> *You shall show me the path of life, in Your Presence is fullness of joy.*
> *Your word is a lamp unto my feet, and a light unto my path.*

The Proverbs also warns us about choosing the right path in life:

> *I have taught you in the ways of wisdom, I have led you in right paths.*
> *The path of the just is as the shining light, that shines more and more unto the perfect day.*
> *Ponder the path of your feet, and let your ways be established.*

I am certain and very confident of one thing. I shall never

choose to wander off from the path that God has set before me. I have no plans to retire from the Lord's work as long as He gives me breath and undertakes. It is not my choice but His that I press on.

David in Psalm 23 ends the Psalm with these words, "Surely goodness and mercy shall follow me all the days of my life: and I will dwell in the house of the Lord forever."

The Apostle Paul, in Acts 20 verse 24, wrote words that I have taken to heart and live by daily: "But none of these things move me, neither count I my life dear unto myself, so that I might finish my course with joy, and the ministry, which I have received of the Lord Jesus, to testify the gospel of the grace of God."

Many saints of God come to the point when they think that there is nothing more they can do with or for God and consequently retire. As long as we can pray, make a telephone call, write a letter or just share a smile and a word with a visitor, we can still do it as unto the Lord.

I remember the Evangelist Dr. Billy Graham once said, "You may not be able to do everything you once did or everything you would like to do. Instead of feeling guilty or frustrated, however, thank God that you can still do some things, and do them faithfully and well."

Jesus is our prime example for working. St. John 5 verse 17 He said, "My Father worketh hitherto, and I work." Then in St. John 17 verse 4 He said, "I have finished the work which Thou gavest me to do."

On the Cross Jesus said, "It is finished," not intimating that through being crucified His life and work was finished. The work of bearing the sins of mankind, and saving all who come in repentance to receive His great and full salvation, was now complete. He now ever lives to pray and intercede for us before His Father's Glory.

Why do I never think of quitting or retiring? Because Jesus said, "I must work the works of Him that sent me, while it is day: for the night cometh, when no man can work." Solemn words indeed from the Master.

I believe we are in the twilight of this present age and we all need to be strong in the grace that is in Christ Jesus.

In Paul's second epistle to Timothy Chapter 3, he warns us of perilous times coming, and I believe we are there now more than ever. We cannot disagree with all the signs that are around us.

"Mankind are lovers of their own selves, covetous, boasters, proud, blasphemers, disobedient to parents, unthankful, unholy. Without natural affection, trucebreakers, false accusers, incontinent, fierce, despisers of those that are good. Traitors, heady, high minded, lovers of pleasures more than lovers of God."

We see the evidence of these things on every side. Many folk say these things have always been present, so what is new? I believe the answer is that sin is given so much publicity nowadays. In times past many did not practice what they preached. By comparison, many now preach what they practice.

In latter years I have often been accused of being old-fashioned and I have need to come into the twenty-first century. My defence is that I serve an old-fashioned God, the Ancient of Days, Who decreed, "I am the Lord Thy God. I change not."

Also I love to serve Jesus, the Son of God, Who is "the same yesterday, today and forever".

The Scriptures and God's Gospel of grace never changes. God is not up for modernisation. His Word is truth. He never relies on gimmicks and jokes. Woe are we if we preach not the Gospel. The entire Word of God is to be preached and not just the favourite parts, and it does well for us to remember that when we meet God we will have to give account of our words, action and service.

With each passing year and visits to a number of churches, I am saddened to see how the Gospel is so much watered down. When we are invited to give our hearts to the Lord, we are led to believe that henceforth life is going to be a bed of roses. That is not the case. "Jesus bids us to take up our Cross and follow Him." A Cross is to be endured, not enjoyed. It is easy to sing "Onward Christian Soldiers" without realising we are in a war against sin and Satan from the beginning.

Neither do I believe there is any salvation without repentance. I cannot recall hearing any service on the subject of repentance for years. I have not heard the Ten Commandments taught since I was at Sunday school.

There is a trend of preachers preaching what they think people want to hear. Some call this tendency "people pleasing". The Bible calls it "itching ears". Folk love flowery sermons all about God's love and what we can receive from Him. This is so much in contrast to important things we also need to consider. Like being taught the Judgements of God and what lies in the future with the Second coming of Christ.

We are without excuse if we neglect so great a salvation and wander from the Word of God. Paul puts it this way in 1 Corinthians 9 verse 16: "For though I preach the gospel, I have nothing to glory of: for necessity is laid upon me, yea; woe is unto me, if I preach not the gospel."

Sharing our Christian testimony, witnessing for Jesus Christ, living the faith and presenting it through the sharing of Scripture is not only expected by God but is to be paramount if we are to convince and convict others through the Holy Spirit.

We often hear the phrase, "Whatever is the world coming to?" or, "Can things get any worse?" Governments and politicians worldwide keep meeting, pontificate, make and break agreements, and argue and go to war. Elaborate plans and legislation are put into place. New laws are introduced with the aim that all man-made plans will benefit all. If only they would return to the Word of God and believe and be led by what it reveals.

Bible prophecies are coming true on a regular basis. The Bible is more up to date than tomorrow's newspaper.

For centuries we have been warned about changes to this planet earth. Thanks be to God that so many are concerned about climate change, carbon emissions, the effect on the nation's health and the environment.

It is so heartening and encouraging to see that more and more individuals and countries are taking strenuous efforts to do their part. We do a great deal about smoke-free zones and then see an amazing volcano that distributes mega-tons of lava and several feet of ash covering extensive areas.

We battle against raging fires, and heat and dams for flooding, and keeping back high tides. Do we know or even care that the Scripture, 2 Peter Chapter 3 verse 10, states very clearly, "But the day of the Lord will come as a thief in the night; in the which the heavens will pass away with a great noise, and the elements shall melt with fervent heat, the earth also and the works that are therein shall be burned up."

The earth belongs to God and we are to do our uppermost to treat it well and with respect.

It is so good to see the millions of trees that are being planted. How so many plastic commodities are replaced or recycled. How fish and birds and wildlife are protected to avoid becoming extinct. God knows all about our struggles and endeavours, but it will not be our will but His that will be done in the end.

Similar to the path of life remains the cycle of human life and existence until we die. However, we should not overlook the fact that we are spiritual beings and God has ordained that our spirits never die but live on after physical death.

The Apostle Paul in 1 Corinthians 15 gave us these challenging words: "It is sown a natural body; it is raised a spiritual body. There is natural body, and there is a spiritual body."

"For this corruptible must put on incorruption, and this mortal must put on immortality. So when this corruptible shall have put on incorruption, and this mortal shall have put on immortality, then shall be brought to pass the saying that is written, Death is swallowed up in victory."

During the season of spring we see the amazing scenes of new life budding all around us, especially here in Great Britain. Speaking personally, I am so glad that this is the time of the year when we remember Good Friday and Easter Day. It is also special for me because my natural birthday is in April. A time of year when we see lighter evenings, the change from dark winter to new and bright spring time.

The appearance of myriads of daffodils, tulips and much welcome spring flowers. The singing of birds at daybreak, bright sunny days, and catkins and leaves appearing on the trees as carpets of grass adorn the fields. All around us is the unfailing evidence of newness of life.

What a picture this also conveys concerning the death of Jesus on the Cross of Calvary on Good Friday, and the glorious new resurrection of Him from the tomb on Easter Day. He no longer lays in a dark tomb but is full of life and raised in resurrection power.

My heart is so full of praise and expectation because Jesus lives. Similarly I rejoice and feel so happy that that new life is shared by so many faithful Christians around the world.

In days of darkness and war and want, we often fail to see all the wonderful things the body of Christ, His Church and other Believers are doing throughout the world.

From friars, monks and nuns who spend long hours in prayer and meditation in spiritual communities. Committed to personal intercession and giving of personal care.

Thousands of very small groups of Christians who continue to support and work in struggling churches and very small congregations. Jesus continues to encourage them with these words, "Fear not, little flock; for it is your Father's good pleasure to give you the kingdom."

Tremendous ministry goes forth within prisons and borstals and youth detention centres. Folk may be grouped together away from communities, but the Lord has His people on hand to minister to them with His gospel. Never failing in His Word: "The Spirit of the Lord is upon me; because the Lord hath anointed me to preach good tidings unto the meek; he hath sent me to bind up the broken hearted, to proclaim liberty to the captives, and the opening of the prison to them that are bound." We are so thankful for all who witness in our prisons.

Conscious that many Christians are praying for the Jews and the Peace of Jerusalem is a delight to our God. This in light of His ancient covenant to Abraham, Isaac and Jacob, and continually through the descendants of the twelve tribes of Israel of His choosing.

Along with many Christians who are praying for persecuted Christians around the world who are martyred, tortured and imprisoned for their faith. We must not forget them in light of Hebrews 13 verse 3: "Remember them that are in bonds, as bound with them: and them that suffer adversity, as being yourselves also in the body."

For the tremendous work going on in youth groups and fellowships, beach missions and city mission work, we give God thanks. Rejoicing too in all that God is doing through faithful and committed missionaries throughout the world.

From baby care to the elderly in nursing and residential homes. Homes where often these folk have been abandoned, neglected or seldom visited even by their closest relatives.

Whatever path God has chosen for us to travel on, we can always be assured that He walks along every inch of the way with us. Truly it is a wonderful way of truth and we can be so blessed as we travel on with the Master.

The Gospel of St. Luke records how a couple walked beside Jesus in the path that led to Emmaus, but they did not recognise Him even as they spoke about Him on the way. Clearly Jesus did not wish at that time for the companions to see Him in the flesh but to see Him in the Scriptures. At the end of the journey, it was only then they realised Jesus had walked beside them all the way, and Luke records that, "Beginning at Moses and all the prophets, He expounded unto them in all the scriptures the things concerning Himself."

Little wonder then that the travellers on that path that day were able to say later, "Did not our heart burn within us, while He talked with us by the way, and while He opened to us the Scriptures?" I do so well understand this realisation and that very same experience. We are never left or forsaken as He journeys with us in life.

Christians look forward to a coming day when we shall no longer be walking in this present path of life. This world is not our home but we are simply passing through it. We are destined for a future where we shall not be walking in muddy and wet or grassy paths but walking in the newness of eternal life on streets that are paved of purest gold.

The joy and privilege of walking these earthly paths with precious Christian brothers and sisters will be eclipsed by living in the Heavenly Presence of Almighty God our Heavenly Father, His Son the Lord Jesus Christ and the Holy Spirit. We will see them as they are!

This is God's doing and it is marvellous in our eyes. By adoption we that are "born again" become heirs of God and joint heirs with Jesus Christ.

With death behind us, eternal life before us, we shall be promoted to glory through being absent from this physical body but present with the Lord.

The Scripture of 1 Corinthians 2 verse 9 confirms, "But as it is written, Eye hath not seen, nor ear heard, neither have entered into the heart of man, the things which God hath prepared for them that love Him." We only have a glimpse of what is to come and our dwelling in the Heavenly accommodation that the Lord has gone on to prepare for us.

The Revelation of the Bible does much more than gladden the heart.

The building of the wall in Heaven is of jasper, the city is of pure gold, like unto clear glass. The foundations of the Heavenly city are garnished with all manner of precious stones; sapphires, topaz and emeralds are mentioned amongst so many others.

A pure river of water of life, clear as crystal, proceeds forth from the throne of God surrounded by a beautiful rainbow. However, I am sure that meeting the Lord Jesus, face to face, will be the greatest joy of all.

There will be no war, death, sickness or tears in Heaven. No pain or parting or sadness because at God's right hand there will be pleasures for evermore.

Just imagine Jesus presenting us to God the Father as though we never sinned according to the Epistle of Jude verse 24: "Now unto Him that is able to keep you from falling, and present you faultless before the Presence of His glory with exceeding joy."

Until then, living in eager expectation of what is to come in glory, I press on knowing what Paul wrote to the church at Corinth: "To the weak became I as weak: I am made all things to all men, that I might by all means save some. And I do this for the gospel's sake."

It is a true story, with a glorious ending, that awaiting around the corner there will everlasting life since death will be swallowed up in victory.

Having walked the entire path in this earthly life, through sunshine and shadow, in good and not so good times, enjoying the companionship of fellow Christians along the way, it will be worth it all when we see Jesus.